DIARY OF A
TOKYO
TEEN

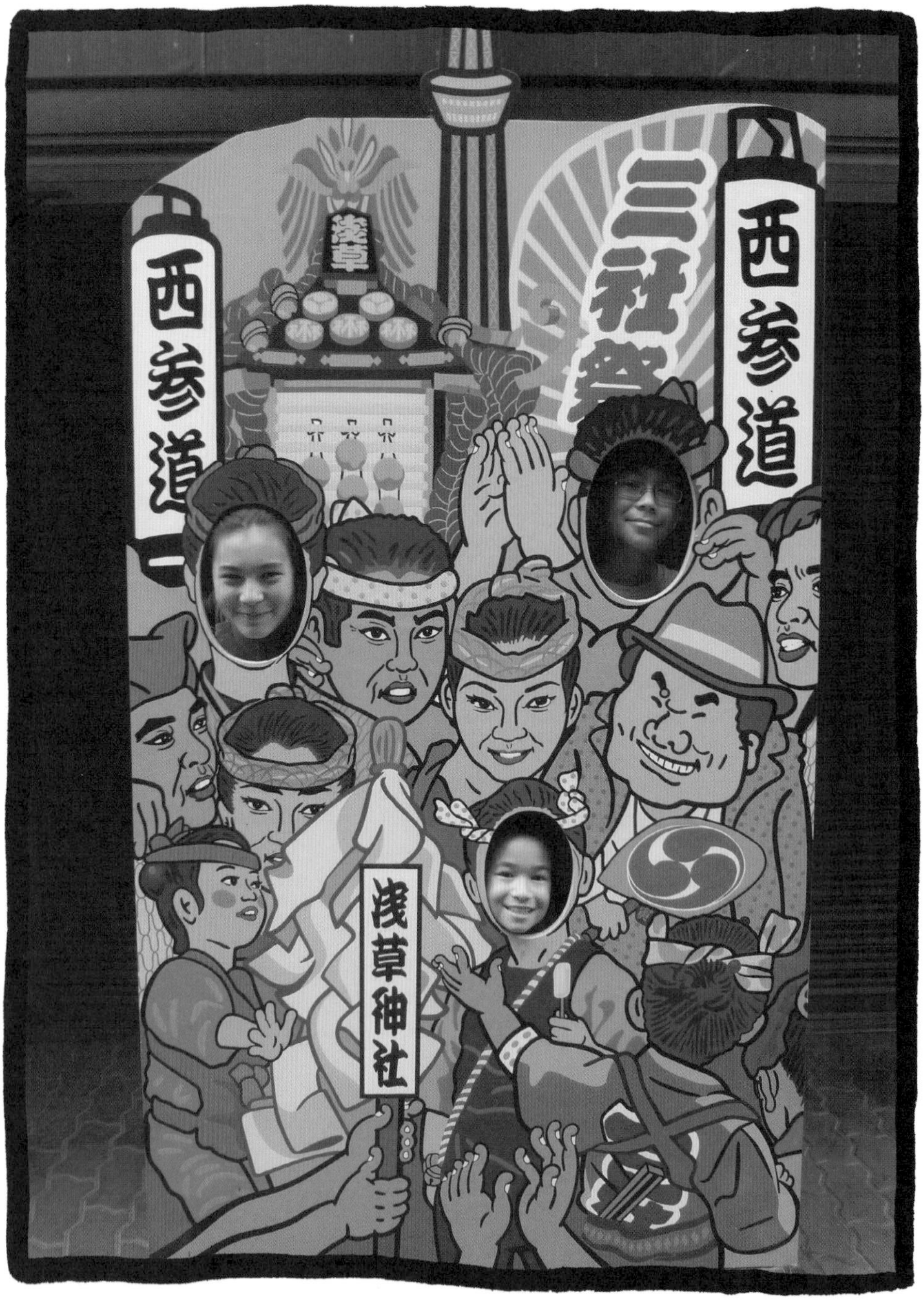
西参道
浅草
三社祭
西参道
浅草神社

DIARY OF A
TOKYO
TEEN

A Japanese-American Girl Travels to the Land of Trendy Fashion, High-Tech Toilets and Maid Cafes

Written and Drawn by

Christine Mari Inzer

TUTTLE Publishing

Tokyo | Rutland, Vermont | Singapore

CONTENTS

OK AS YOU CAN TELL I CAN'T DRAW ANIME/ MANGA VERY WELL...

I'd take the Chiyoda line to...

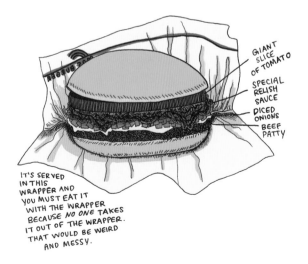

GIANT SLICE OF TOMATO

SPECIAL RELISH SAUCE

DICED ONIONS

BEEF PATTY

IT'S SERVED IN THIS WRAPPER AND YOU MUST EAT IT WITH THE WRAPPER BECAUSE NO ONE TAKES IT OUT OF THE WRAPPER. THAT WOULD BE WEIRD AND MESSY.

A maiko is an apprentice geisha. They get invited to entertain at parties, primarily dancing.

THIS THING AT THE TOP IS A GOLDEN PHOENIX.

ON THIS LEVEL YOU CAN SEE THE INTERIOR.

SOYBEANS!

Fried shrimp TEMPURA EBI

CUCUMBER

EDAMAME

EGG

MORE TEMPURA These are fried onions and really small shrimp

HAM

CARROT

SOMEN

CHICKEN

NOODLES x3

FRIED BEAN CURD

TAKO

YAKITORI

IKA

SAKANA

"ART BALLET" DANCERS: THEY WEREN'T EVEN THAT GOOD AT DANCING BUT THEY HAD AWESOME COSTUMES. EVERYBODY WAS WONDERING WHAT ART BALLET MEANT. TURNED OUT TO BE BELLY DANCING WITH INDIAN MUSIC?

INTRODUCTION

DURING THE SUMMER OF 2013, JUST BEFORE I TURNED 16, I SPENT EIGHT WEEKS IN JAPAN VISITING MY GRANDPARENTS AND GETTING REACQUAINTED WITH MY BIRTHPLACE.

WHILE IN JAPAN, I VISITED MY FAVORITE SPOTS IN TOKYO THAT I HADN'T SEEN IN YEARS, AND I ALSO TRAVELED TO KYOTO FOR THE FIRST TIME.

JAPAN IS A FASCINATING MIX OF THE OLD AND THE NEW: ANCIENT TEMPLES AND MODERN SKYSCRAPERS, GEISHA AND MAID CAFES, ENKA AND J-POP, SUSHI AND MOSBURGER.

I EXPERIENCED ALL OF THESE THINGS IN JAPAN, AND I LEARNED A LOT ABOUT MYSELF ALONG THE WAY. IT WAS AN INCREDIBLE JOURNEY, AND WITH THIS BOOK I HOPE TO SHARE IT WITH YOU.

BABY CHRISTINE AREN'T I CUTE?

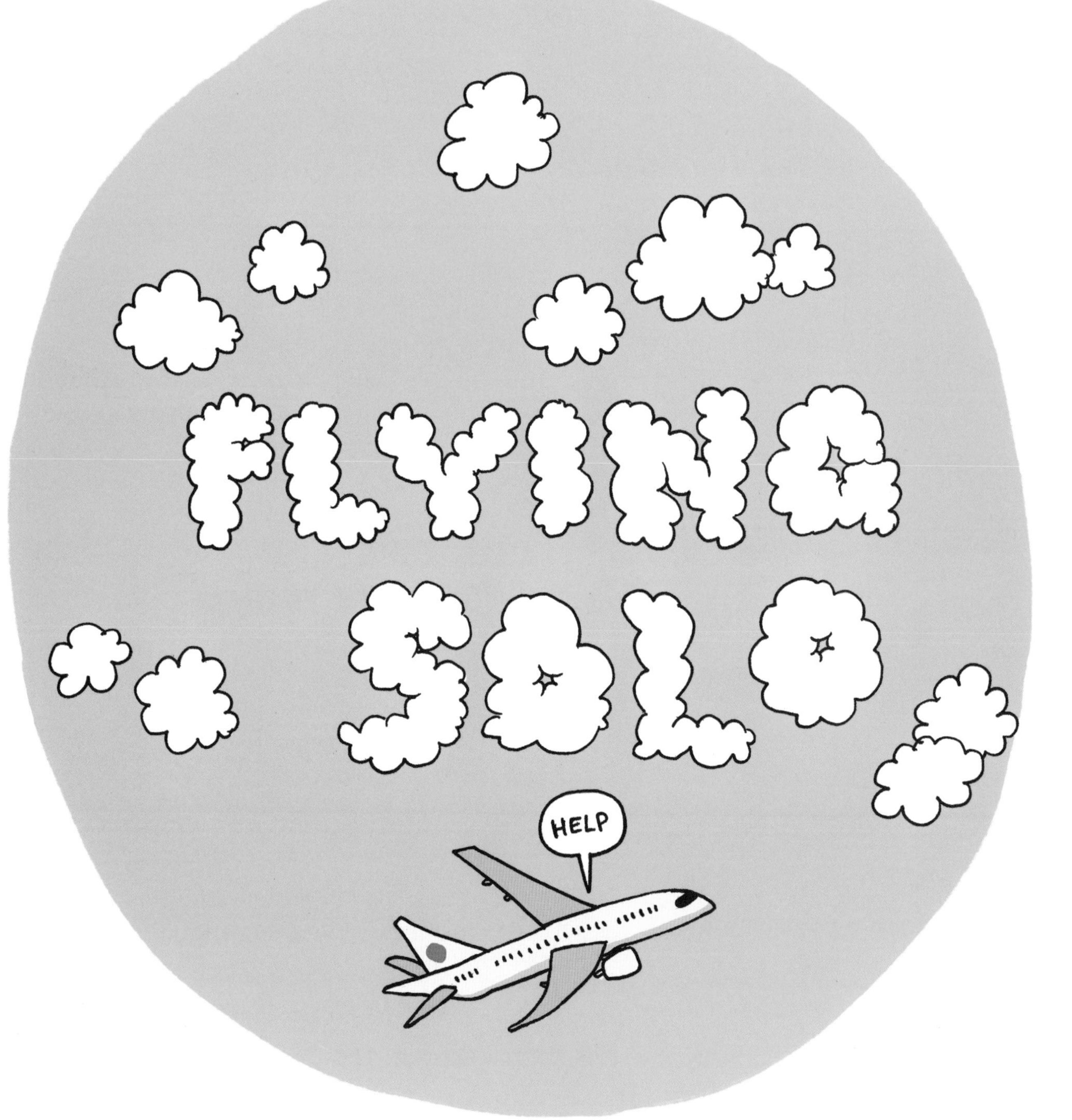
FLYING SOLO
HELP

Each day is a journey, and the journey itself home.

– Matsuo Bashō,
The Narrow Road to the Deep North

THIS IS IT.

I'M AT THE AIRPORT. I'VE CHECKED MY BAG AND I'M GETTING READY TO SAY GOODBYE TO MY FAMILY.

DARK BROWN HAIR

SOME ARTSY FARTSY SHIRT

BRAND NEW BACKPACK!

↑ SWATCH

SHAPELY YOGA PANTS

NEW CONVERSE!

UP IN the air

I HAD A TRANSCENDENTAL MOMENT ON THE PLANE, EATING MY HÄAGEN-DAZS ICE CREAM AND LISTENING TO CAMILLE SAINT-SAENS' DANSE MACABRE.

The ice cream was very hard

OH, BY THE WAY, I'M ON THE PLANE RIGHT NOW.
IT'S REALLY HARD TO TELL WHAT TIME OF DAY IT IS, AND I CAN'T SLEEP.

IT'S STILL 7 HOURS TILL THE PLANE ARRIVES, BUT I'M ALREADY WONDERING WHAT I'M SUPPOSED TO DO WHEN I GET OFF THE PLANE (MY DAD TRIED TO WALK ME THROUGH IT, BUT I FORGOT WHICH ORDER IT'S SUPPOSED TO GO IN).

IF I SPOKE JAPANESE BETTER, I WOULD NOT BE AS ANXIOUS (ALTHOUGH I GET ANXIOUS EASILY).

EARLIER I WAS WORRIED ABOUT THE PLANE TOILETS (see illust. for further explanation)

The toilet is so small

Me in toilet

PRESSURE

THIS IS TAKING SO LONG

I'M JEALOUS B/C MY SEAT NEIGHBOR LOOKS SO PEACEFULLY ASLEEP

10

The Traveler

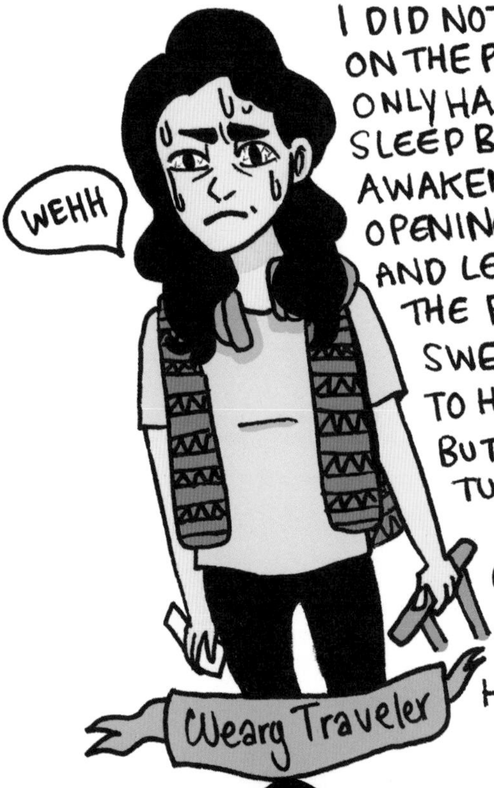
WEHH
Weary Traveler

I DID NOT SLEEP ON THE PLANE... I ONLY HAD ONE HOUR OF SLEEP BEFORE BEING AWAKENED BY PASSENGERS OPENING WINDOW SHADES AND LETTING LIGHT FLOOD THE PLANE. I AM TIRED, SWEATY, AND FIGHTING TO HOLD BACK MY FEAR. BUT GETTING OUT TURNS OUT TO BE REALLY EASY... THE CUSTOMS OFFICIAL BARELY GLANCES AT MY PASSPORT BEFORE HE WELCOMES ME TO JAPAN.

OVERALL, I HAD BEEN HOPING FOR A MORE GLAMOROUS ENTRANCE, BUT I COULDN'T EVEN ROLL MY SUITCASE PROPERLY. THIS IS WHAT I WANTED

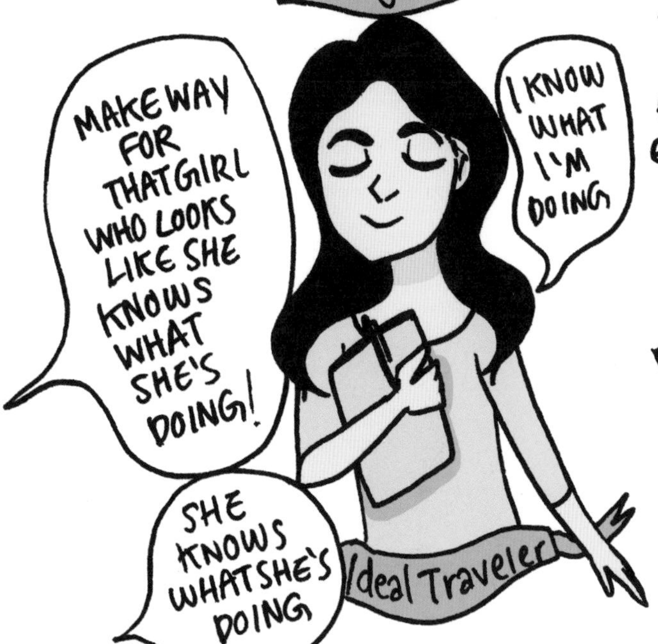
MAKE WAY FOR THAT GIRL WHO LOOKS LIKE SHE KNOWS WHAT SHE'S DOING!
I KNOW WHAT I'M DOING
SHE KNOWS WHAT SHE'S DOING
Ideal Traveler

THE ARRIVAL GATE AT NARITA

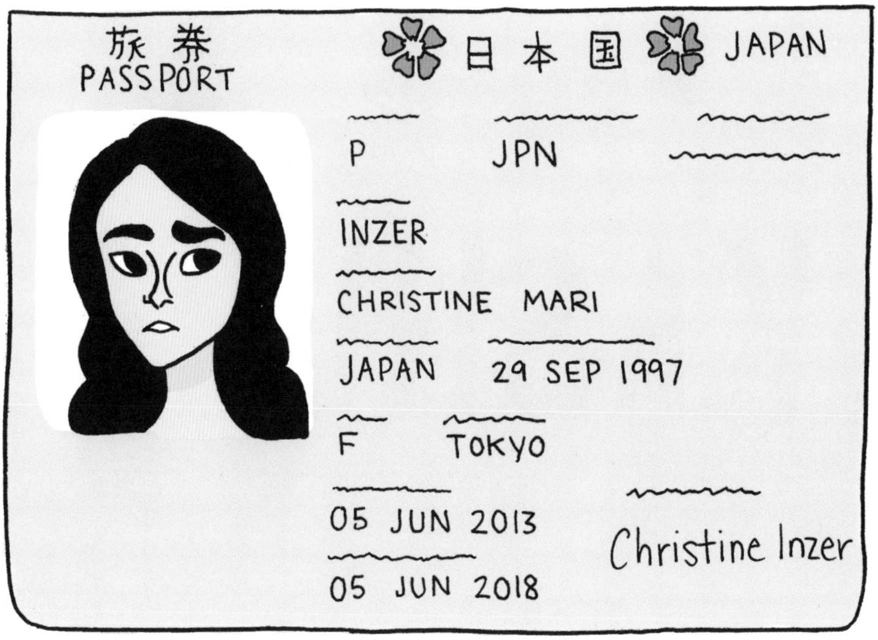
旅券
PASSPORT
日本国
JAPAN
P
JPN
INZER
CHRISTINE MARI
JAPAN
29 SEP 1997
F
TOKYO
05 JUN 2013
05 JUN 2018
Christine Inzer

I HAVE TWO PASSPORTS. I HAVE TO USE MY JAPANESE ONE WHEN I ENTER JAPAN, AND MY USA ONE WHEN I RETURN TO AMERICA. I'M IN CONSTANT FEAR OF LOSING ONE, OR BOTH, OF THEM.

STARTING IN...

KASHIWA

柏

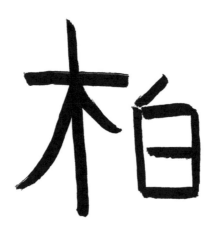

KASHIWA IS WHERE MY GRANDPARENTS
LIVE. IT'S A SMALL CITY JUST
OUTSIDE OF TOKYO.

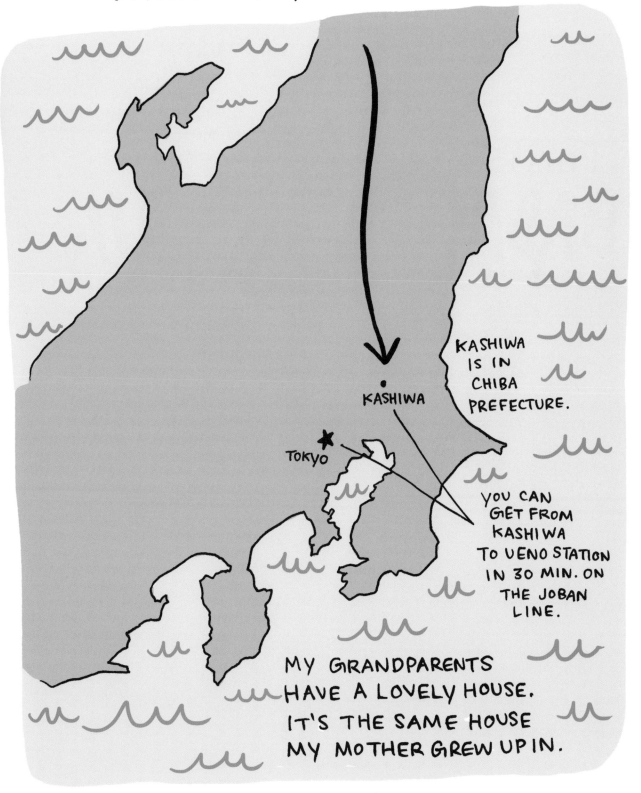

KASHIWA
IS IN
CHIBA
PREFECTURE.

KASHIWA

TOKYO

YOU CAN
GET FROM
KASHIWA
TO UENO STATION
IN 30 MIN. ON
THE JOBAN
LINE.

MY GRANDPARENTS
HAVE A LOVELY HOUSE.
IT'S THE SAME HOUSE
MY MOTHER GREW UP IN.

This is BABA

MY GRANDMA.

AND THIS IS JI JI

WHILE I WAS IN JAPAN, I STAYED WITH MY GRAND-PARENTS. BABA AND I, AS YOU'LL SEE IN THIS BOOK, DID ALMOST EVERY-THING TOGETHER.

MY GRANDPA. EVERY SUMMER HE GOES OFF INTO THE YAMAGATA MOUNTAINS FOR A FEW WEEKS TO COOL OFF AND GO FISHING.

BABA

JIJI

THE BEST AMERICAN FAST FOOD ISN'T
EVEN IN AMERICA.

Yum Yum Yum

BESIDES MY GRANDPARENTS, THE SECOND GREATEST REUNION I HAD IN JAPAN WAS WITH A CERTAIN FAST FOOD CHAIN YOU CAN'T FIND IN AMERICA...

MOS BURGER

THE LOVE OF MY LIFE. I'LL SHOW YOU WHAT A MOS BURGER IS:

GIANT SLICE OF TOMATO

SPECIAL RELISH SAUCE

DICED ONIONS

BEEF PATTY

IT'S SERVED IN THIS WRAPPER AND YOU MUST EAT IT WITH THE WRAPPER BECAUSE NO ONE TAKES IT OUT OF THE WRAPPER. THAT WOULD BE WEIRD AND MESSY.

SPEAKING OF BURGERS, THE FAST FOOD SERVICE IN JAPAN CAN BE BEST DESCRIBED AS A MIRACLE. THE EMPLOYEES ARE ANGELS, IN MY EYES.

We are patient as hell, attentive, and enthusiastic And we won't screw your order up.

IT'S ALWAYS AMAZED ME — HOW MUCH A PERSON'S ATTITUDE CAN ALTER THE NATURE OF THEIR JOB. HERE IN JAPAN, THERE'S AN ENTHUSIASM AND DEDICATION IN EMPLOYEES THAT I'VE NEVER EXPERIENCED ANYWHERE ELSE.

I HAVE SO MUCH RESPECT FOR THESE PEOPLE.

IT'S MY THIRD DAY

MY AUNT AND COUSINS ARE HERE. THEIR NAMES ARE MEGU, TAIGA & KAREN. THEY'RE LIVING IN INDIA RIGHT NOW AND ARE VISITING TOO. I'M TOLD I'M A LOT LIKE MY AUNT MEGU. WE'RE BOTH VERY DIFFERENT FROM MY MOTHER (AKA MEGU'S OLDER SISTER, AYUMI) AND I THINK THAT MAKES US SIMILAR TOO. MY MOTHER IS LESS... CONVENTIONAL.

MEGU
- FAIRER
- TALLER
- SLENDER
- LIVES IN INDIA
- TAKES AFTER MOTHER
- THE GOOD CHILD

AYUMI
- TANNER
- SHORTER
- ATHLETIC
- LIVES IN USA
- TAKES AFTER FATHER
- TROUBLEMAKER

YOU REALLY WOULDN'T THINK THEY WERE PRODUCED BY THE SAME TWO PEOPLE, BUT I LIKE IT THIS WAY. IT MAKES LIFE MORE INTERESTING.

TRENDY TEENAGERS

I WENT TO THE KASHIWA STATION MALL WITH BABA TODAY.
IT HAS ONE BUILDING WITH A LOT OF STORES FOR YOUNG, HIP
PEOPLE, AND I REALLY LIKE IT. IT'S CHEAP TOO.
IT WAS VERY INTIMIDATING THOUGH TO
STAND AROUND THE GIRLS WORKING THERE.

THIS HAT STYLE IS POPULAR

AND OF COURSE THEY HAVE PERFECTLY DYED, SHINY HAIR AND LOADS OF EYE MAKE-UP

VIVID GRAPHIC TEES

I BOUGHT a bag that says California despite having no connection to the state whatsoever. I'd be flattered if someone thinks I'm a ❀ Cali gurl ❀

SAW A GIRL WEARING THIS FOR REAL

THIS IS THE BEST OUTFIT I BROUGHT.

FLOWER JEANS ARE EVERY-WHERE

OF COURSE THEY WEAR HEELS! THEY TOWERED OVER ME... UGH!

23

EVEN THOUGH I WAS IN JAPAN
DURING THE SUMMER, SCHOOLS
WERE STILL LARGELY IN SESSION.
AS A RESULT, I LOOKED EVEN
MORE OUT OF PLACE BECAUSE THIS
MEANT EVERYONE MY AGE IS IN
A UNIFORM OF SOME SORT...

THE あさごはん CLUB

OH, AND MAKE BEAT TAKESHI THE PRINCIPAL, ALWAYS.

meet the cousins

THESE TWO CUTIES ARE MY AUNT MEGU'S CHILDREN... THEIR NATURAL FLUENCY IN JAPANESE MAKES ME FEEL INCOMPETENT NEXT TO THEM!

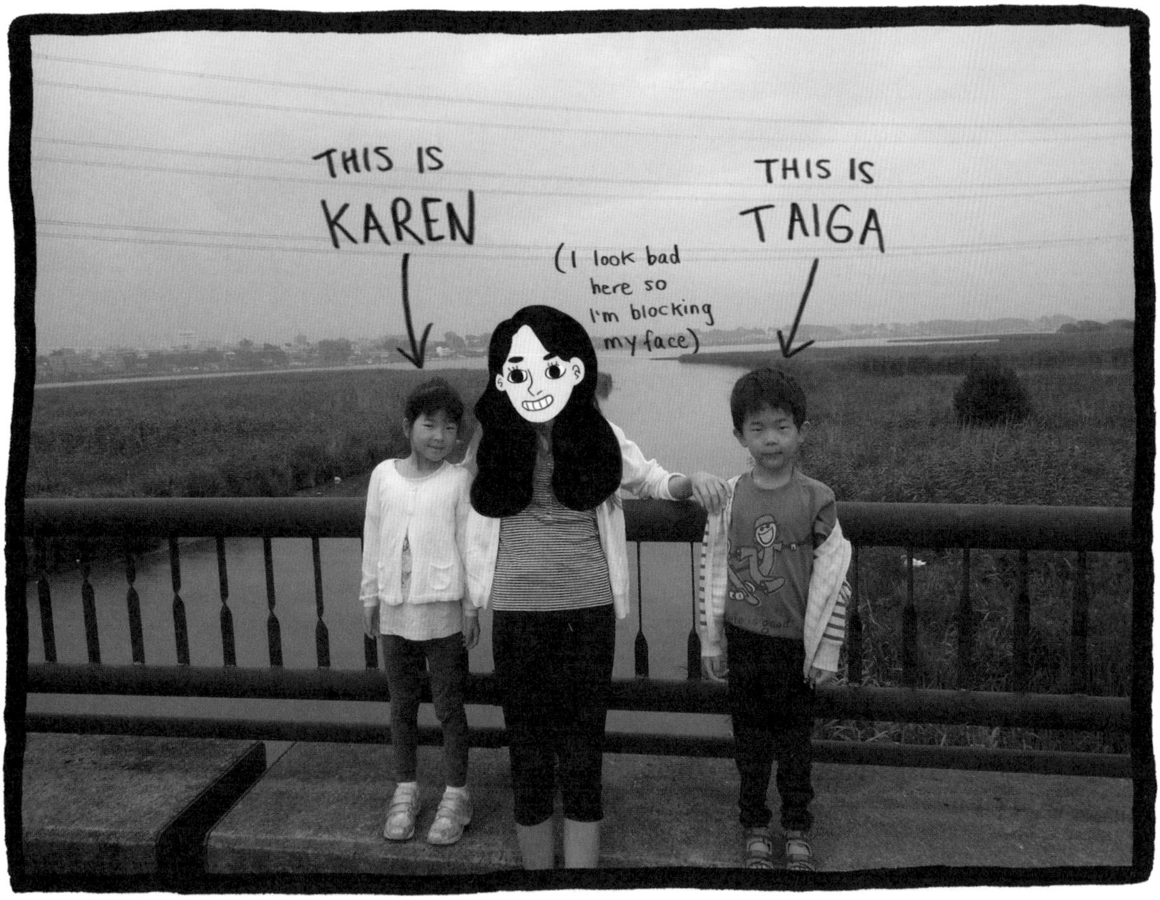
THIS IS KAREN
(I look bad here so I'm blocking my face)
THIS IS TAIGA

JAPANESE TV IS A HELL OF AN EXPERIENCE.

IN THE LAST FEW DAYS, I HAVE WATCHED TELEVISION SHOWS IN WHICH I SAW:

- TWO PEOPLE WEARING MASCOT COSTUMES BUNGEE JUMP OFF OF A BRIDGE
- JAPANESE TV CELEBRITIES DOUSING THEMSELVES IN LUBRICANT AND PUSHED DOWN A GIANT SLIP N SLIDE
- A MAN STRIP DOWN TO HIS UNDERWEAR AND HIDE UNDER VARIOUS PIECES OF FURNITURE

THIS IS ALL REALITY TELEVISION, JUST BY THE WAY.

Popular TV personalities:

THIS COMEDIAN WHO PAINTS ON THICK EYEBROWS AND DRESSES LIKE A SCHOOLGIRL

ROLA-CHAN IS... ER.... HOW DO I PUT THIS? SHE'S INESCAPABLE. KNOWN FOR HER DISTINCT VOICE, SHE'S ALL OVER TV. (SHE DRIVES ME CRAZY.)

THIS GUY!!!

I SEE HIM ALL THE TIME BUT I DON'T KNOW WHO HE IS, SO I REFER TO HIM AS BOWL CUT MAN

MATSUKO DELUXE, A CROSS DRESSING TV PERSONALITY

BECKY, A HALF JAPANESE CELEBRITY KNOWN FOR HER GREEN EYES (HEY, I'M HALF TOO. PUT ME ON TV, DAMN IT!)

THERE'S ALSO ALWAYS THAT ONE YOUNG GUY WITH ANIME HAIR

THERE'S TONS OF THESE, THOUGH

TYPES OF SHOWS YOU SEE ON JAPANESE TELEVISION:

1.) The popular comedy shows where a panel of TV personalities watch other celebrities do weird things.

2.) Nature shows that are just long montages of beautiful imagery coupled with traditional music or piano. (Jiji watches this)

3.) Intense period dramas.

4.) Intense modern dramas.

5.) Medical shows that reenact a weird medical incident, sort of like a reality House M.D., I guess...?

6.) My favorite - the travel shows. They just send people somewhere and make them do stuff. Sometimes funny, sometimes serious.

BATHTIME

AKA THE ONE ELEMENT OF JAPANESE CULTURE I COULDN'T HANDLE

LOOK, HERE'S THE THING. IN JAPAN, YOU DON'T EVER TAKE BATHS **LIKE THIS:**

THERE ISN'T ANY SOAP IN THE TUB. YOU DO NOT WASH YOURSELF IN. THE. TUB.

INSTEAD, YOU WASH YOURSELF OUTSIDE THE TUB. **LIKE THIS:**

① RINSE SELF BY POURING A BUCKET OF WATER ON SELF

② LATHER SOAP ON SELF LIKE A SUPERSTAR

③ RINSE AGAIN— DUMP THAT WATER BUCKET OVER SELF

YOU DO ALL OF THIS BEFORE YOU GET INTO THE TUB.

I TRIED TO DO IT.

DRENCHED IN WATER

BUT HERE'S WHAT THEY DON'T TELL YOU...

IT'S SO **COLD**

LUCKY FOR ME, MY GRANDPARENTS ALSO HAD A SHOWER.

HYSTERICAL IN HARAJUKU

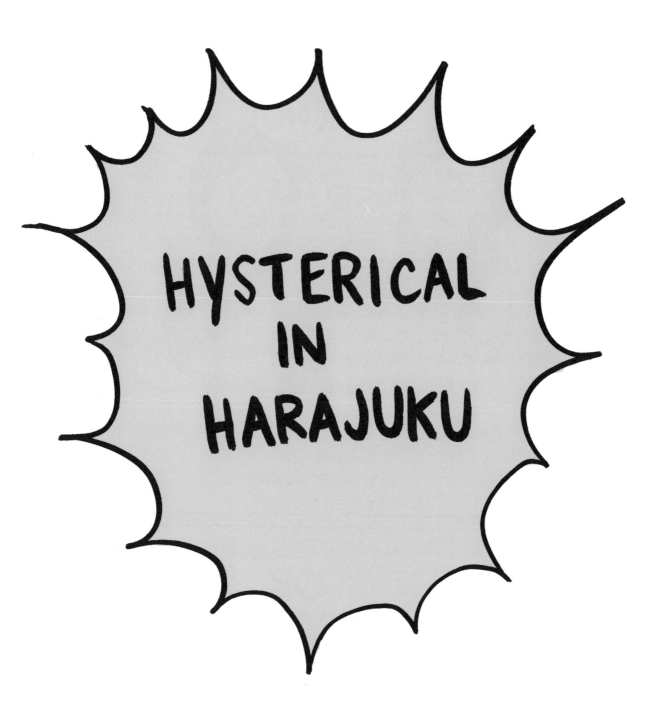

I WANTED

TO GO INTO THE CITY—
BY MYSELF.
AT FIRST, MY GRANDMA
SAID
BUT
I SAID

NO

YES!

I'M
BIG
ENOUGH!

I'VE SEEN
8-YEAR-OLDS
BOARD THE
TRAIN...
I CAN DO
IT, FOR SURE.
AFTER SOME
COAXING BY MY
MOM, MY GRANDMA
SAID **OK**
EVEN THOUGH I
KNOW SHE THOUGHT
I WOULD GET LOST,
GET KIDNAPPED,
GET HURT, GET
MURDERED!??!!
BRING IT.
BUT WHERE DO I GO...?

原宿

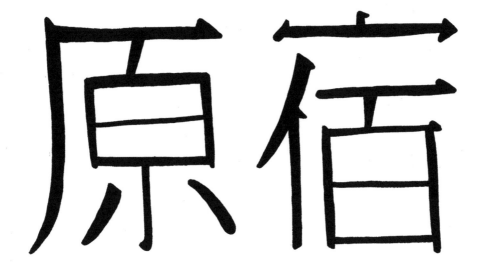

(HARAJUKU)

KASHIWA IS ALL THE WAY UP HERE!

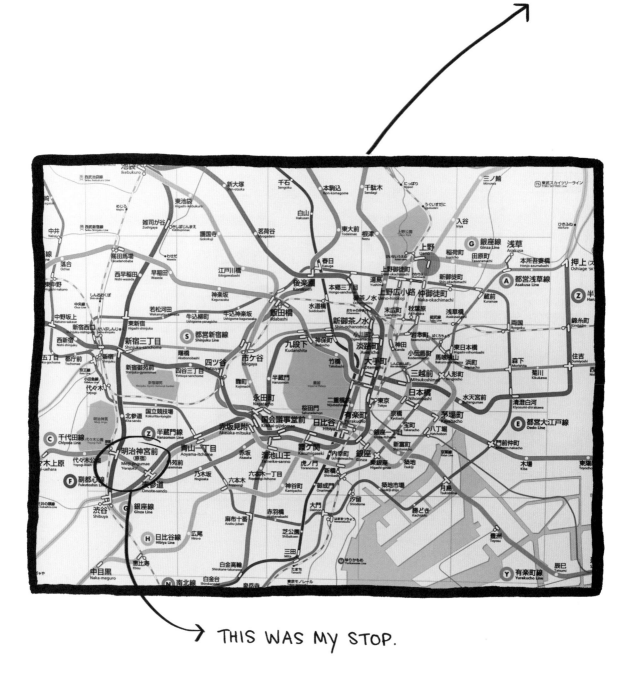

THIS WAS MY STOP.

WE DECIDED ON HARAJUKU, BECAUSE IT WAS EASY TO GET TO AND DIDN'T HAVE MANY "CREEPY" PEOPLE, WHICH WAS MY GRANDMOTHER'S MAIN CONCERN...

THE PLAN WAS (PRETTY) SIMPLE.

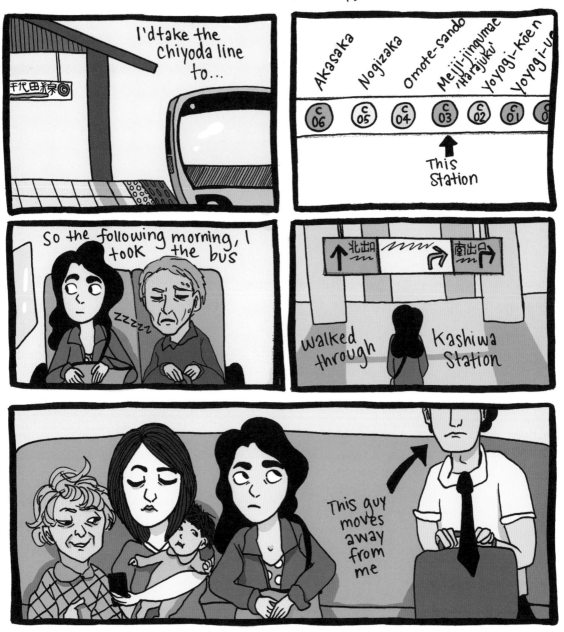

AND THEN I WAS ON THE TRAIN, REALIZING THERE WAS NO TURNING BACK —!

YES, THE SUBWAYS REALLY ARE THIS CLEAN.

NOW STOPPING

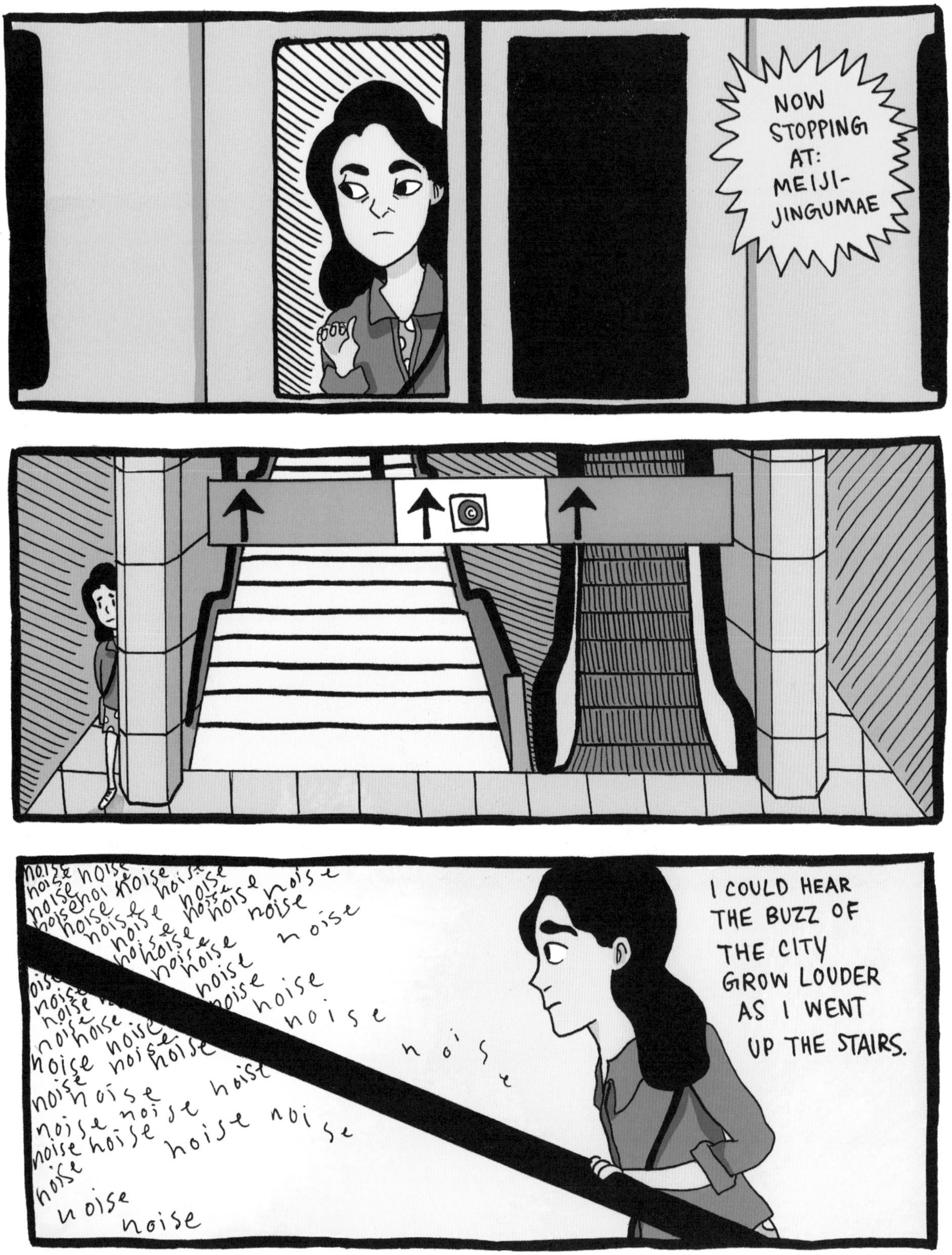
NOW STOPPING AT: MEIJI-JINGUMAE
noise
I COULD HEAR THE BUZZ OF THE CITY GROW LOUDER AS I WENT UP THE STAIRS.

THIS IS HARAJUKU STATION.

IT IS OVER 100 YEARS OLD AND MORE THAN
70,000 PEOPLE PASS THROUGH IT EVERY DAY.

WHEN I GOT OFF THE TRAIN AT HARAJUKU STATION, I NEEDED TO USE THE BATHROOM. I STUMBLED INTO THE FIRST STALL AND ···

SECOND STALL···

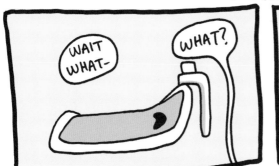

THIRD STALL (there's only 4)

THEN AND NOW

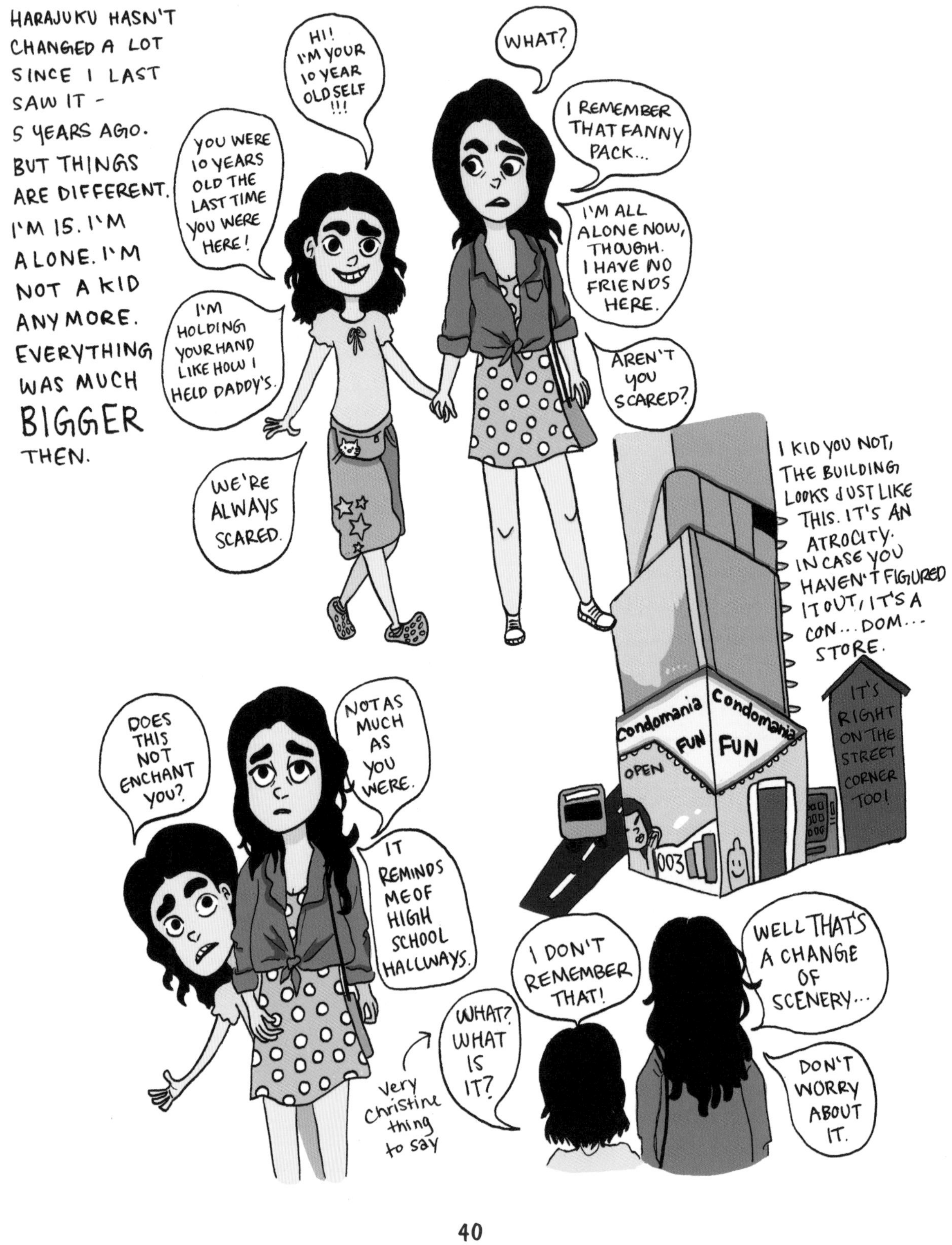
HARAJUKU HASN'T CHANGED A LOT SINCE I LAST SAW IT - 5 YEARS AGO. BUT THINGS ARE DIFFERENT. I'M 15. I'M ALONE. I'M NOT A KID ANYMORE. EVERYTHING WAS MUCH BIGGER THEN.
HI! I'M YOUR 10 YEAR OLD SELF !!!
WHAT?
YOU WERE 10 YEARS OLD THE LAST TIME YOU WERE HERE!
I REMEMBER THAT FANNY PACK...
I'M ALL ALONE NOW, THOUGH. I HAVE NO FRIENDS HERE.
I'M HOLDING YOUR HAND LIKE HOW I HELD DADDY'S.
AREN'T YOU SCARED?
WE'RE ALWAYS SCARED.
I KID YOU NOT, THE BUILDING LOOKS JUST LIKE THIS. IT'S AN ATROCITY. IN CASE YOU HAVEN'T FIGURED IT OUT, IT'S A CON... DOM... STORE.
Condomania
Condomania
FUN
FUN
OPEN
003
IT'S RIGHT ON THE STREET CORNER TOO!
DOES THIS NOT ENCHANT YOU?
NOT AS MUCH AS YOU WERE.
IT REMINDS ME OF HIGH SCHOOL HALLWAYS.
I DON'T REMEMBER THAT!
WELL THAT'S A CHANGE OF SCENERY...
WHAT? WHAT IS IT?
Very Christine thing to say
DON'T WORRY ABOUT IT.

YES, THIS PLACE ACTUALLY EXISTS.

TAKESHITA DORI

TAKESHITA-DORI IS A FAMOUS STREET IN HARAJUKU
LINED WITH FASHION BOUTIQUES WHERE ALL THE
YOUNG TRENDY PEOPLE GO TO SHOP.

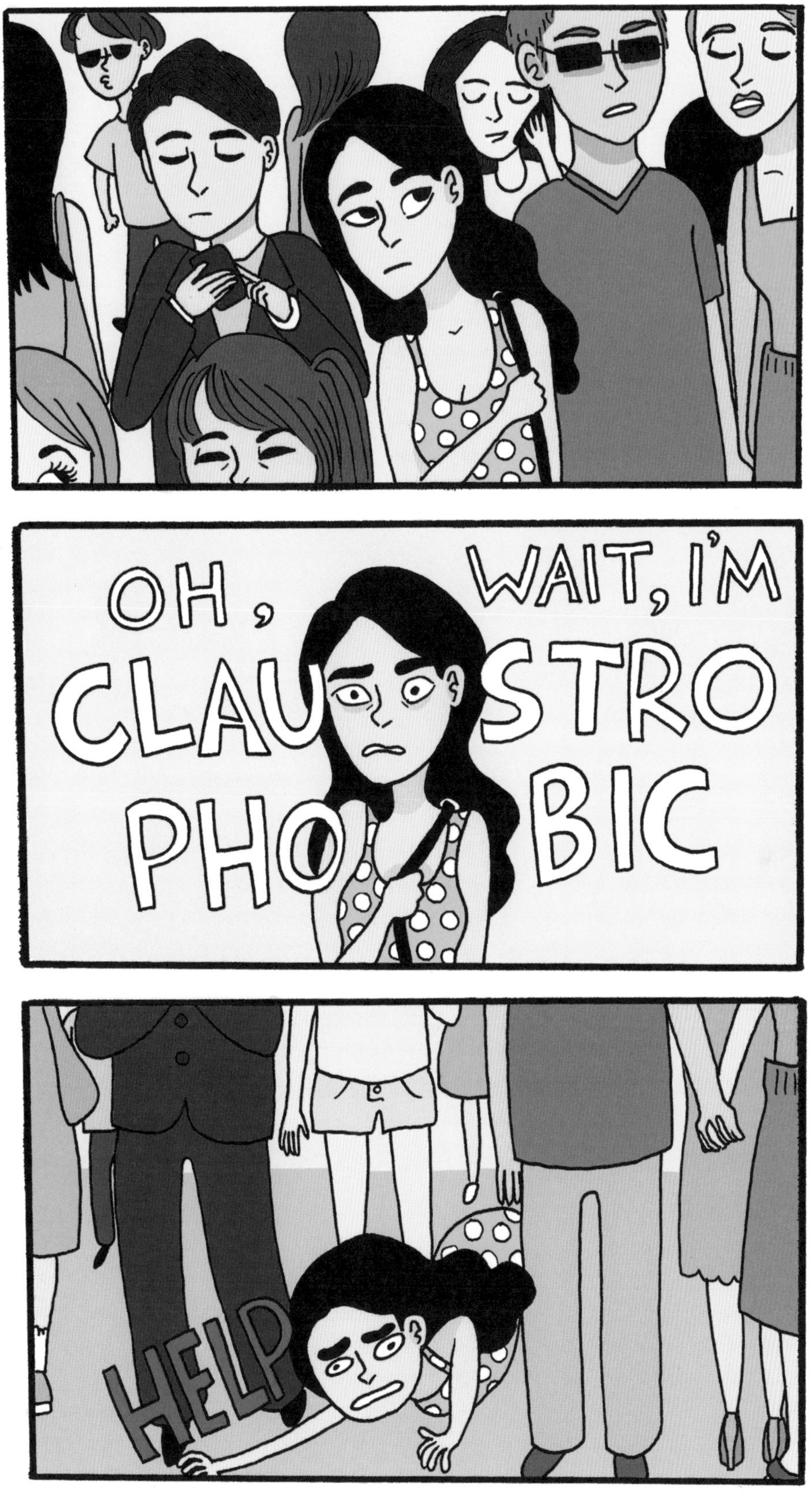
OH, WAIT, I'M
CLAUSTROPHOBIC
HELP

THAT'S ME WHEN I WAS TEN. I DON'T THINK THINGS HAVE CHANGED MUCH SINCE THEN.

WHEN I WAS YOUNGER, THE SHOPS AT TAKESHITA DORI WERE A SOURCE OF FASCINATION AND WONDER. MANY OF THE CLOTHES THESE STORES SOLD ALWAYS HAD AN AURA AROUND THEM THAT MADE THEM SEEM FORBIDDEN TO REGULAR PEOPLE LIKE ME...

I WISH MOM WOULD LET US WEAR THIS STUFF!

...I'M GLAD THAT SHE DOESN'T...

fashion show

JAPANESE STREET STYLE HAS SO MANY DIFFERENT CATEGORIES, BUT I WANTED TO SHOWCASE SOME BY DESIGNING VARIANTS OF MY OWN OUTFIT

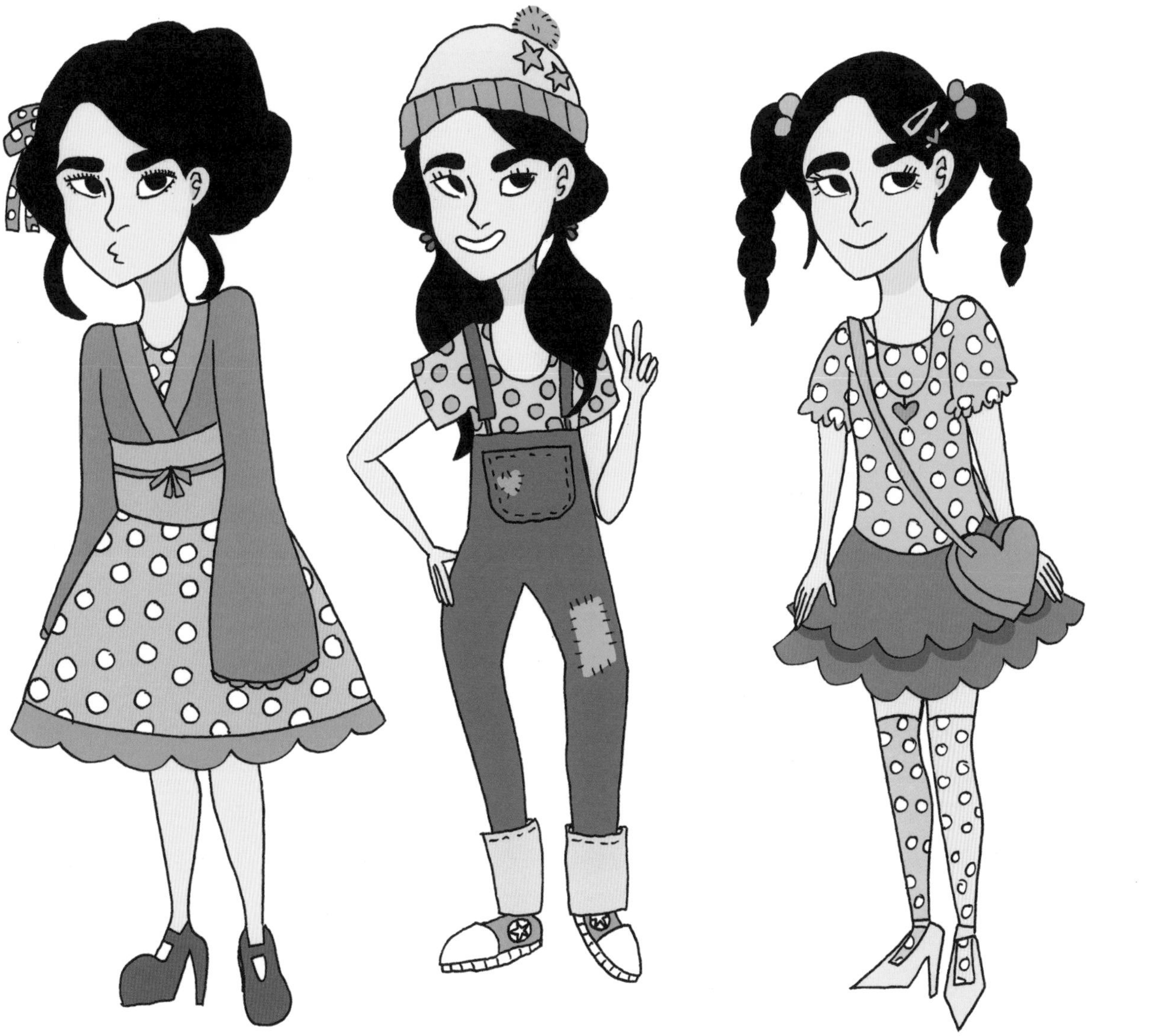

IN JAPAN, AS YOU CAN SEE, FOOD IS MORE
THAN NOURISHMENT — IT'S AN ART.

TOKYO CREPES

COFFEE JELLY

APPLE CINNAMON

DON'T WANT FRUIT? GET CHEESECAKE & ICECREAM & CREAM AND THEY'LL DRIZZLE CHOCOLATE ALL OVER IT

PEACHES & CREAM AND ICE CREAM

CREAM & CHOCOLATE

STRAWBERRIES & CREAM

BANANAS & CREAM AND ICE CREAM & CHOCOLATE

KIWIS & CREAM

CUSTARD

BLUEBERRY

DON'T WANT SWEET? GET TUNA SALAD AND LETTUCE

STRAWBERRY & BLUEBERRY AND ICE CREAM

MANGO & CREAM

CHOCOLATE

BANANA & ICE CREAM AND MORE CHOCOLATE

ALMOND & CHOCOLATE

GREEN TEA ICE CREAM AND RED BEAN

RED BEAN PASTE

STRAWBERRY CHEESE CAKE

If YOU VISIT HARAJUKU AND WALK DOWN **TAKESHITA DORI,** YOU WILL STUMBLE ACROSS SOME BIG PINK CREPERIES!!! YOU SHOULD DO SOME GOOD AND **REWARD** YOURSELF BY BUYING A FRESH DELICIOUS **crepe!** AND YOU'LL NEVER HAVE TO WORRY ABOUT HAVING ENOUGH OPTIONS...

49

MODEL SCOUT OR PERVERT ?

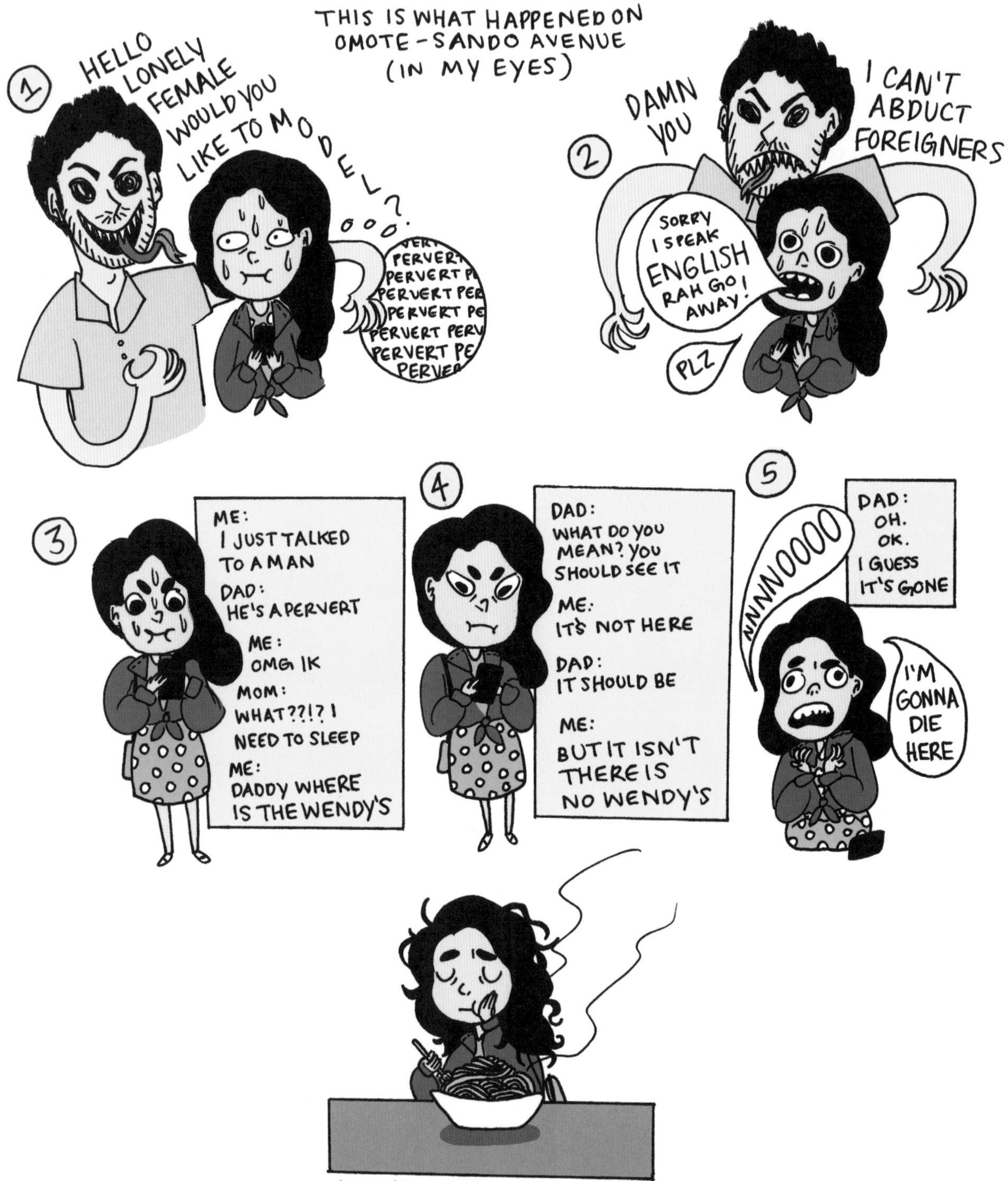
THIS IS WHAT HAPPENED ON OMOTE-SANDO AVENUE (IN MY EYES)
1
HELLO LONELY FEMALE WOULD YOU LIKE TO MODEL?
ooo.
PERVERT PERVERT PERVERT PERVERT PERVERT PERVERT PERVERT PERVERT
2
DAMN YOU
I CAN'T ABDUCT FOREIGNERS
SORRY I SPEAK ENGLISH RAH GO! AWAY!
PLZ
3
ME: I JUST TALKED TO A MAN
DAD: HE'S A PERVERT
ME: OMG IK
MOM: WHAT??!?! NEED TO SLEEP
ME: DADDY WHERE IS THE WENDY'S
4
DAD: WHAT DO YOU MEAN? YOU SHOULD SEE IT
ME: IT'S NOT HERE
DAD: IT SHOULD BE
ME: BUT IT ISN'T THERE IS NO WENDY'S
5
DAD: OH. OK. I GUESS IT'S GONE
NNNNOOOO
I'M GONNA DIE HERE

AND THEN I ATE A HEAPING PLATE OF SPAGHETTI THAT REMINDED ME A LITTLE OF MY MOM.

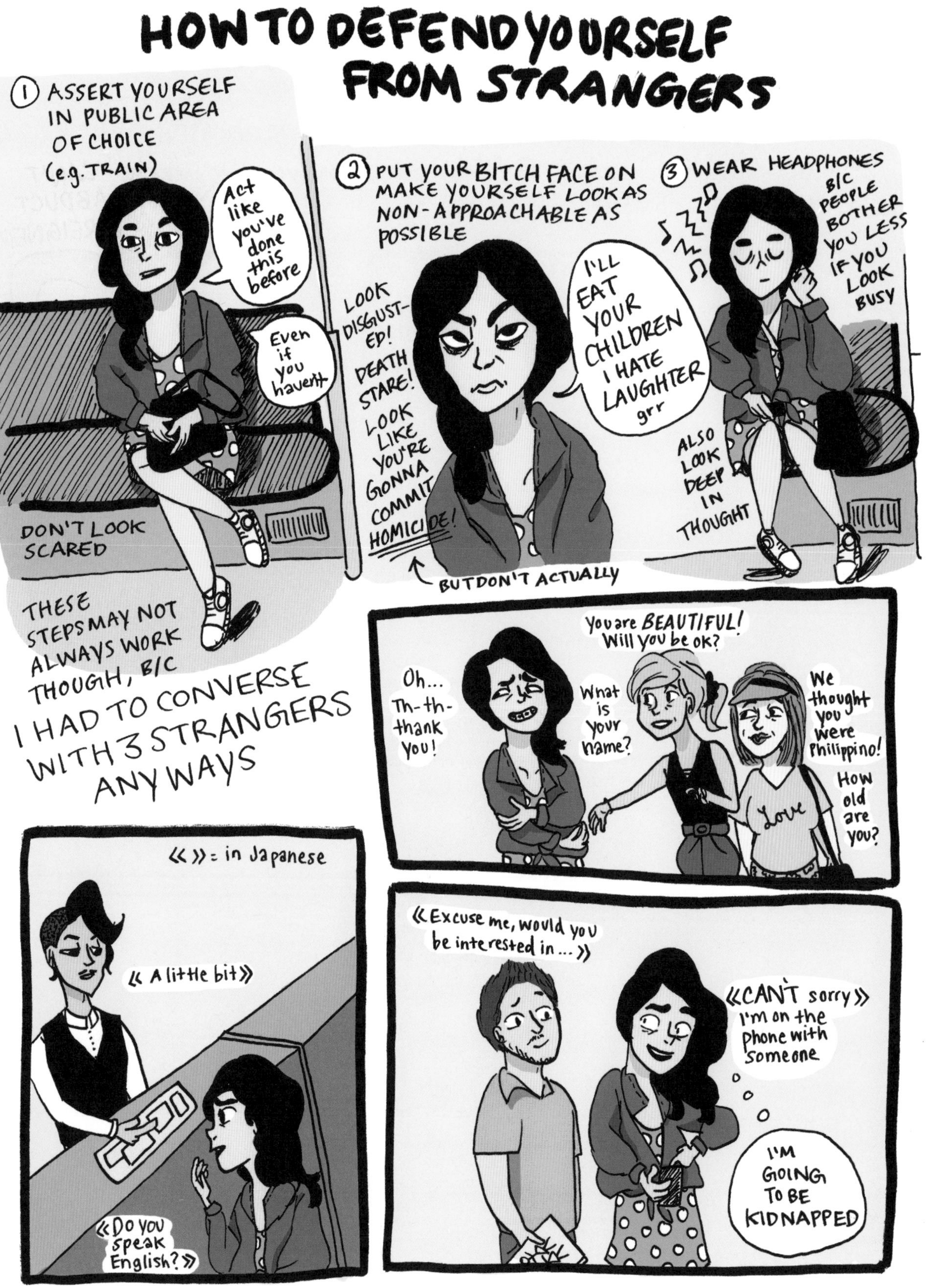
HOW TO DEFEND YOURSELF FROM STRANGERS
① ASSERT YOURSELF IN PUBLIC AREA OF CHOICE (e.g. TRAIN)
Act like you've done this before
Even if you haven't
DON'T LOOK SCARED
② PUT YOUR BITCH FACE ON MAKE YOURSELF LOOK AS NON-APPROACHABLE AS POSSIBLE
LOOK DISGUST-ED! DEATH STARE! LOOK LIKE YOU'RE GONNA COMMIT HOMICIDE!
BUT DON'T ACTUALLY
I'LL EAT YOUR CHILDREN I HATE LAUGHTER grr
③ WEAR HEADPHONES
B/C PEOPLE BOTHER YOU LESS IF YOU LOOK BUSY
ALSO LOOK DEEP IN THOUGHT
THESE STEPS MAY NOT ALWAYS WORK THOUGH, B/C
I HAD TO CONVERSE WITH 3 STRANGERS ANYWAYS
You are BEAUTIFUL! Will you be ok?
Oh... Th-th-thank you!
What is your name?
We thought you were Philippino!
How old are you?
Love
«»= in Japanese
« A little bit »
«Do you speak English?»
«Excuse me, would you be interested in...»
«CAN'T sorry» I'm on the phone with someone
I'M GOING TO BE KIDNAPPED

YOU KNOW, WHEN I FIRST SET OFF FOR HARAJUKU BY MYSELF, I HAD THOUGHT THAT THE EXPERIENCE WAS GOING TO BE MY GLAMOROUS TRANSITION INTO ADULTHOOD. I WANTED TO FEEL STRONG AND INDEPENDENT. BUT THAT ISN'T WHAT HAPPENED. IF ANYTHING, IT MADE ME REALIZE HOW YOUNG I STILL WAS, HOW LONELY I FELT, AND HOW MUCH I MISSED MY PARENTS...

... BUT MOST OF ALL, IT REMINDED ME THAT I'M STILL A KID.

OF THIS WHOLE ADVENTURE, I THINK COMING HOME WAS MY FAVORITE PART.

Chasing Maiko in KYOTO

THE BULLET TRAIN IS AN EXPERIENCE IN ITSELF.

A RIDE ON THE shinkansen
新幹線

ALSO KNOWN AS THE BULLET TRAIN! MY GRANDMOTHER AND I RODE IT TO GET TO KYOTO, AND IT ONLY TOOK THREE HOURS. IF WE USED A NORMAL TRAIN, IT WOULD HAVE TAKEN MUCH LONGER. THE INTERIOR IS ALSO OBVIOUSLY A LOT NICER.

I LIKED THE VIEW. MAINLY JUST ROOFTOPS OF SMALL HOUSES AND STRETCHES OF GREEN FARM-LAND AND MOUNTAINS. BUT WE DIDN'T GET TO SEE MT. FUJI BECAUSE IT WAS TOO CLOUDY!

THERE WAS A BUSINESS MAN ACROSS THE AISLE WHO LOOKED VERY TIRED AND UPSET

YOU CAN FIND BEAUTY ANYWHERE IN KYOTO,
EVEN IN QUIET SIDE STREETS LIKE THIS ONE.

WHAT I ATE TODAY

AFTER WE ARRIVED IN KYOTO, BABA AND I CHECKED INTO OUR HOTEL AND FOUND A NICE TONKATSU PLACE NEARBY. TONKATSU IS A POPULAR DISH IN JAPAN, CONSISTING OF BREADED PORK SERVED WITH CABBAGE AND A SPECIAL SAUCE.

BOILED WATER

½ TOAST SLICE

2 CASTELLA BALLS

CASTELLA'S A KIND OF SWEET BREAD, BUT IT'S USUALLY IN RECTANGLE FORM.

CHICKEN SOBA

KYOTO STYLE!

KYOTO STYLE IS A LIGHTER BROTH. TOKYO STYLE IS DARK + HEAVIER.

♡ KATSUDON ♡

BREADED PORK + EGG OVER RICE

CABBAGE

CLAM MISO

TOKYO PERSON
This has NO taste!
KYOTO SOUP

KYOTO PERSON
This is too SALTY!
TOKYO SOUP

JAPANESE CULTURE IS JUST WAY TOO CUTE TO HANDLE SOMETIMES. THE UNIFORMS AT THE TONKATSU PLACE WERE SO NICE. I LIKE HOW THEY WEAR UNIFORMS WITH PRIDE AND SEEM FULL OF ENERGY.

IT WAS FUNNY TO SEE THE ELEGANT HOTEL EMPLOYEE SLING MY VIBRANT GIRLY BACKPACK OVER HIS SHOULDER.

HE REMINDED ME OF CHRISTOPHER WALKEN.

TWO OF MY FAVORITE JAPANESE DISHES ARE:

TONKATSU

BREADED PORK CUTLET WITH RICE

+

AND **KATSUDON**

WHICH IS BREADED PORK ON
TOP OF RICE, WITH EGG AND ONION

EVEN THE PHOTO DOESN'T DO KATSUDON JUSTICE; IT'S SOMETHING YOU HAVE TO EXPERIENCE FIRST-HAND.

ON OUR FIRST FULL DAY IN KYOTO,
MY GRANDMOTHER AND I
WENT TO

KINKAKU-JI

ALSO KNOWN AS THE
"TEMPLE OF THE GOLDEN PAVILION".
IT IS A ZEN BUDDHIST TEMPLE,
FAMOUS FOR ITS SHINING GOLDEN
EXTERIOR AND ITS GARDEN LAYOUT.

THIS THING
AT THE TOP
IS A GOLDEN
PHOENIX.

ON THIS
LEVEL
YOU CAN
SEE
THE INTERIOR.

IF YOU SQUINT, YOU'LL BE ABLE TO SEE THE PHOENIX ON TOP!

ONE OF MY FAVORITE IMAGES OF KINKAKU-JI IS WHEN YOU CAN SEE ITS GOLDEN REFLECTION IN THE WATER.

THIS IS A CLOSE-UP OF THE GOLDEN PHOENIX ON TOP OF KINKAKU-JI:

KIND OF CREEPY LOOKING, NO...?

WHEN I REMARKED ON HOW NEW KINKAKU-JI LOOKED, I LEARNED THE KINKAKU-JI I WAS LOOKING AT WAS A **RECONSTRUCTION.** THE ORIGINAL WAS **BURNED DOWN** BY A CRAZY BUDDHIST MONK.

DRAWN AT THE KINKAKUJI
TEMPLE

IT WAS REALLY CROWDED.
THERE WERE LOTS OF SCHOOL
GROUPS VISITING.

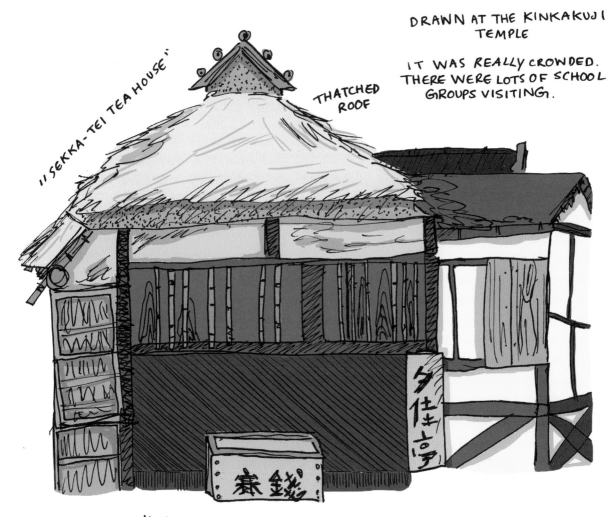

"SEKKA-TEI TEA HOUSE"

THATCHED
ROOF

I'M PRETTY SURE I COMMITTED A BUDDHIST
CRIME TODAY THOUGH WHILE TRYING TO
DRAW THIS:

AN ANT CRAWLED
ONTO MY LEG AND
I FREAKED OUT
AND KILLED IT.

GOMEN.

63

NEXT: RYOANJI

outline of some of the rocks

I THINK I SHOULD TRY AND DO SOME TRANSCENDENTAL THINKING/WRITING, BEING IN ONE OF JAPAN'S MOST FAMOUS HISTORICAL SIGHTS, BUT THE CAMERA CLICKS AND TOURISTS (I KNOW, I KNOW, I'M ONE MYSELF) MAKE IT KIND OF HARD TO BE ENLIGHTENED.

I'M NOT GOING TO TRY AND DRAW THE ROCK GARDEN. IT'S SOMETHING YOU HAVE TO SEE FOR YOURSELF. THERE ARE 15 ROCKS. FROM WHERE I SIT I CAN COUNT 13.
NOW SOMEONE JUST SAID THERE ARE 14.
NOPE, THERE ARE 15.

I'M SUPPOSED TO FEEL GOD OR BUDDHA'S SPIRIT. WHAT DO I SEE?

- I SEE THE PROFILE OF A MAN'S FACE
- I CAN DEFINITELY SEE THE ROCKS AND MOSS AS ISLANDS IN A GRAVEL OCEAN
~ A FOOT?
- I'M NOT VERY GOOD AT THIS
- APPARENTLY YOU'RE SUPPOSED TO BE IN A ZEN STATE TO VIEW THE ROCK GARDEN CORRECTLY SO WOOPS

PEOPLE I'VE SEEN REPEATEDLY TODAY

YOUNG JAPANESE COUPLE ON THE BUS

SCHOOLGIRL I THINK I SCARED AND I FEEL BAD

PERSON I CAN ONLY RECOGNIZE BY HER CLOTHES

RED SKIRT & CROCS

FABULOUS KOREAN BOYS - I SAW ONLY THE BACK OF THEIR HEADS

THIS GUY'S COLLAR WAS POPPED UP

64

THERE ARE A LOT OF THESE DRY LANDSCAPE GARDENS (KARESANSUI) IN KYOTO AND ELSE-WHERE IN JAPAN. THIS IS THE MOST FAMOUS ONE.

THE ROCKS OF RYOANJI

THIS IS A WALL
WHAT DO THE ROCKS LOOK LIKE TO ME?
...ROCKS
IT'S SO HOT. WHAT AM I SUPP-OSED TO BE THINK-ING ABOUT?
THE ROCKS
WILL I BE ABLE TO PUBLISH THIS?
I COULD EASILY BE MORE FAMOUS THAN THE KARDASHIANS.
WHAT LANGUAGE ARE THEY SPEAKING?
OH, IT'S GOTTA BE FRENCH.
OH NO! THE TOUR GROUPS ARE COMING.
I FAIL AT BEING JAPANESE.
WHAT WOULD HAPPEN IF I FELL INTO THE ROCKS?
I ONLY COUNTED 14 ROCKS.
THERE'S SUPPOSED TO BE 15.
WHAT DO YOU SEE IN THE ROCKS?
NOTHING. I SEE NOTHING.

AFTER OBSERVING THE ROCK GARDEN AT RYOANJI, BABA AND I TOOK A WALK AND CAME ACROSS A LARGE POND WITH LOTUSES AND LILYPADS.

Lotus & lilypads from the Landscape Garden

AFTER AN EXHAUSTING DAY TOURING KYOTO, IT WAS NICE TO STOP AND TAKE A MOMENT TO SIMPLY ENJOY WHAT WAS IN FRONT OF ME.

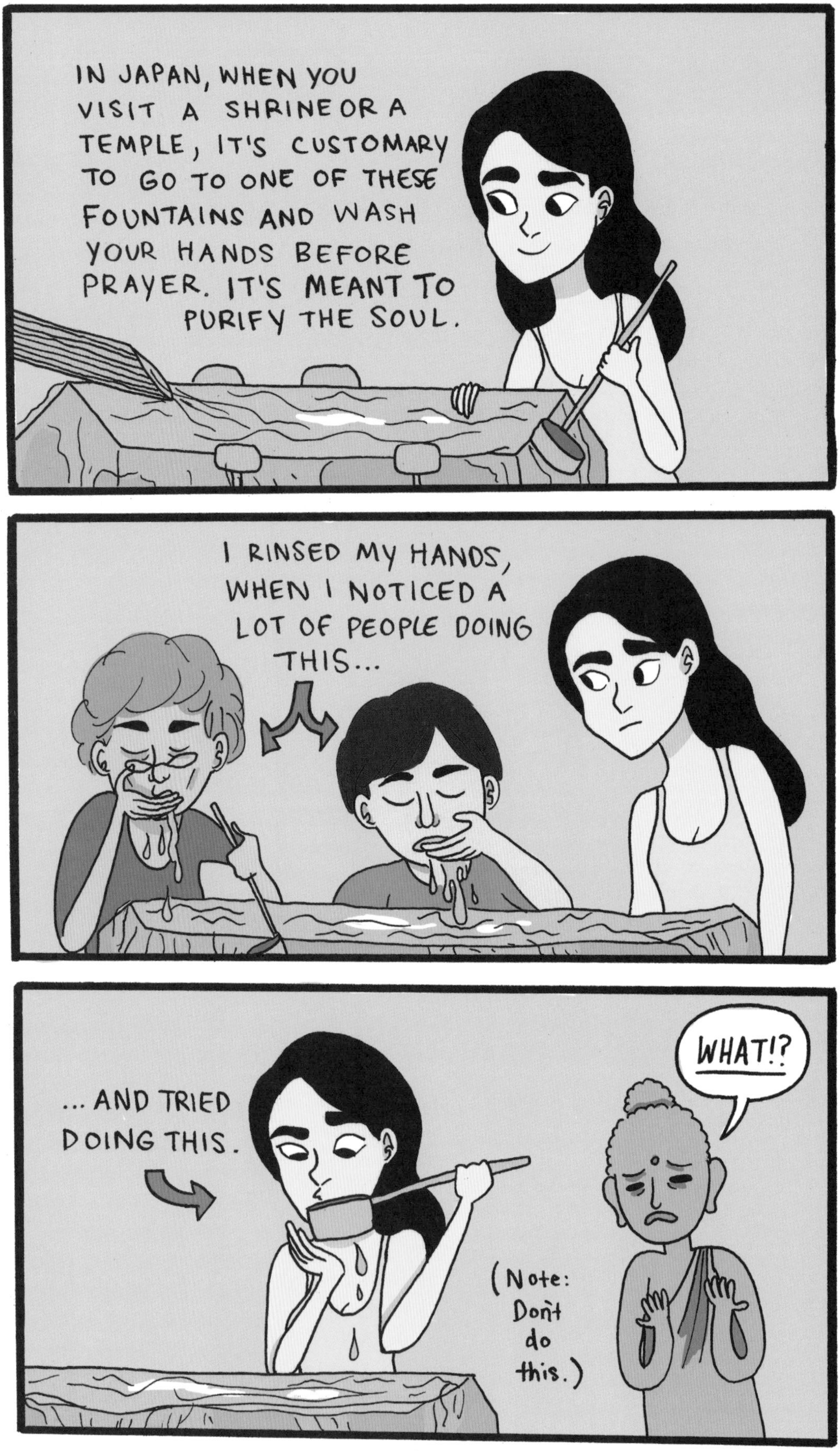
IN JAPAN, WHEN YOU VISIT A SHRINE OR A TEMPLE, IT'S CUSTOMARY TO GO TO ONE OF THESE FOUNTAINS AND WASH YOUR HANDS BEFORE PRAYER. IT'S MEANT TO PURIFY THE SOUL.
I RINSED MY HANDS, WHEN I NOTICED A LOT OF PEOPLE DOING THIS...
...AND TRIED DOING THIS.
(Note: Don't do this.)
WHAT!?

ME, PRETENDING TO KNOW WHAT I'M DOING

ON HOT SUMMER DAYS, THE COOL WATER IS A WELCOMING AND REFRESHING SIGHT.

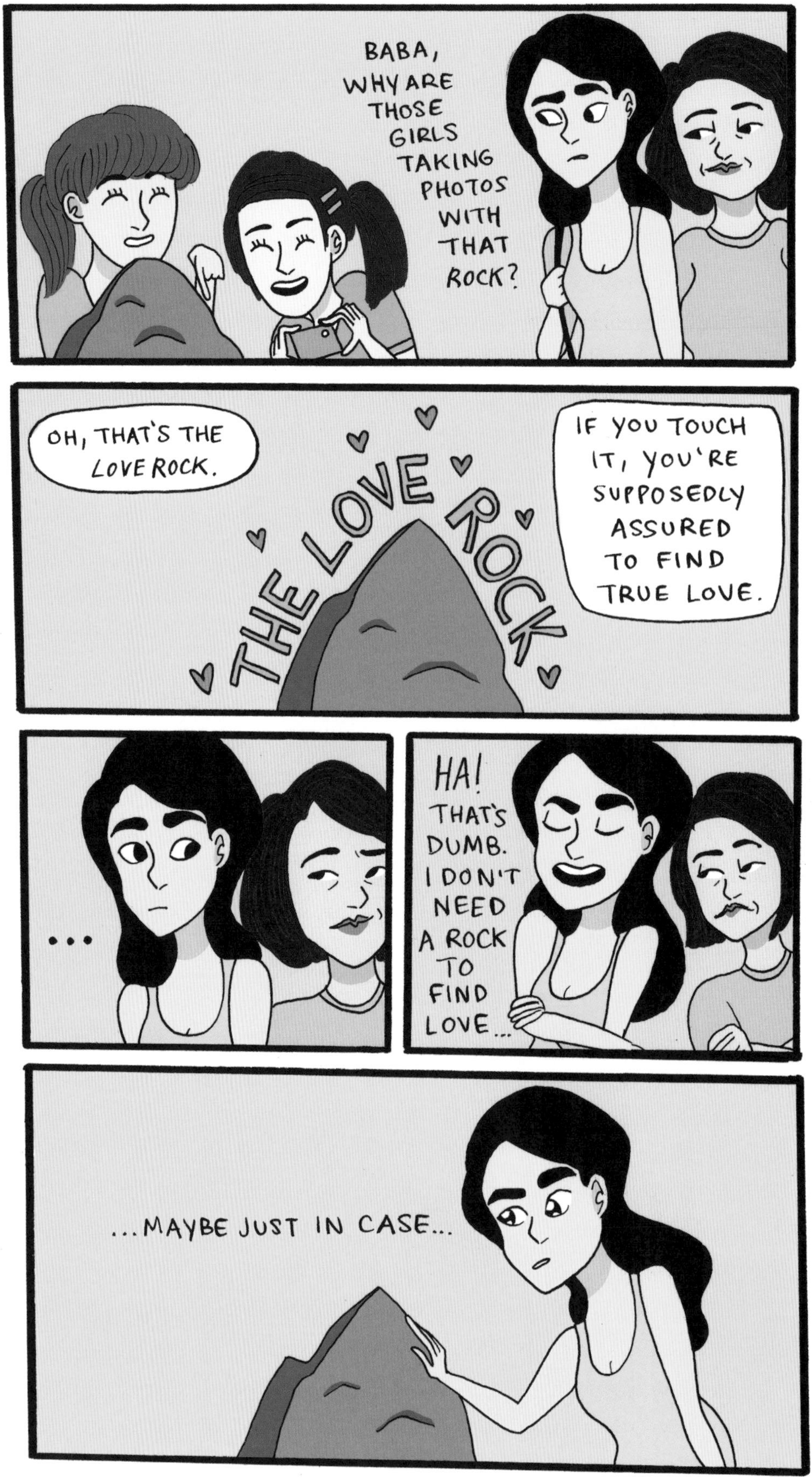
BABA, WHY ARE THOSE GIRLS TAKING PHOTOS WITH THAT ROCK?
OH, THAT'S THE LOVE ROCK.
THE LOVE ROCK
IF YOU TOUCH IT, YOU'RE SUPPOSEDLY ASSURED TO FIND TRUE LOVE.
...
HA! THAT'S DUMB. I DON'T NEED A ROCK TO FIND LOVE...
...MAYBE JUST IN CASE...

THERE ARE TWO OF THESE — YOU'RE SUPPOSED
TO WALK FROM ONE TO THE OTHER WITH
YOUR EYES CLOSED. IT'S A LITTLE COMPLICATED...

THOSE CLOGS (GETA) DIDN'T SLOW HER
DOWN AT ALL!

I FOUND THE GEISHA!

THE GION DISTRICT IN KYOTO IS ONE OF THE FEW PLACES IN JAPAN WHERE YOU CAN SEE A GEISHA. IN THE EARLY EVENING, IF YOU'RE IN THE RIGHT PLACE, YOU CAN SPOT THEM WALKING TO THE OCHAYA (TEAHOUSES) WHERE THEY ENTERTAIN.

MY DAD TOLD ME IT WAS ESSENTIAL TO SEE A GEISHA WHEN IN KYOTO. HE SEARCHED ONLINE AND TOLD ME I MIGHT HAVE LUCK NEAR THE TATSUMI-BASHI BRIDGE. SO IN THE EARLY EVENING, BABA AND I WAITED THERE, CAMERAS IN HAND.

HAVING NO LUCK AT THE BRIDGE, WE WALKED TO HANAMIKOJI STREET, AND VOILA, THE GEISHA APPEARED. TO BE CORRECT, THEY WERE ACTUALLY MAIKO, OR APPRENTICE GEISHA.

I KNEW IN ADVANCE THAT THEY WERE GOING TO WALK QUICKLY, BUT NOW I REALIZE IT'S NOT TO GET TO THEIR APPOINTMENTS ON TIME, BUT TO NOT BE MOBBED BY TOURISTS LIKE ME WHO WANT THEIR PHOTO.

There is the maiko that will sort of acknowledge your presence and faintly smile and look super pumped.

There is also the sort of scary maiko that simply looks down and walks down the street and ignores everything.

MAIKO MAYHEM

A maiko is an apprentice geisha. They get invited to entertain at parties, primarily dancing.

Many young girls who wish to take the first step to geisha-dom audition for JNTM

JAPAN'S NEXT topmaiko

I'M TYRA BANKS & THIS IS CYCLE 10 OF...

YOU MUST HOLD THIS SCALDING HOT TEA CUP FOR 30 MIN

WORK IT! C'MON! BE FIERCE!

Beat Takeshi also hosts the annual Geisha Games, where Maikos must out-beautify (or kill) each other. Winner becomes Japan's most respected geisha.

Everything in this comic is 100% true.

NARA

(1 HOUR FROM KYOTO)

IN NARA, MY GRANDMA AND I WENT TO SEE THE
DAI BUTSU - AKA GIANT BUDDHA - AT TŌDAI-JI TEMPLE.
IF YOU EVER VISIT NARA, YOU WILL EVENTUALLY
COME HERE BECAUSE *EVERYBODY* DOES. IT IS PACKED.
I'D DRAW THE BUDDHA, BUT THAT
WASN'T THE MOST EXCITING EVENT
OF THIS VISIT - IT WAS THIS PILLAR.

LITERALLY IT'S JUST A NORMAL PILLAR,

EXCEPT YOU'RE SUPPOSED TO CRAWL THROUGH THIS NARROW HOLE.

THERE WAS A BIG LONG LINE
OF PEOPLE WAITING TO GO
THROUGH IT SO
NATURALLY...

CHEESE!

MY GRANDMA TOLD
ME THAT CRAWLING
THROUGH IT WAS GOOD LUCK,
SO I DID IT BUT
LATER WE FOUND A MONK
AND QUESTIONED HIM ABOUT
THE PILLAR'S SIGNIFICANCE...

BELIEVE IT OR NOT, THERE'S A HUGE LINE OF
PEOPLE BEHIND ME WAITING TO DO THIS.

BABA AND THE MONK

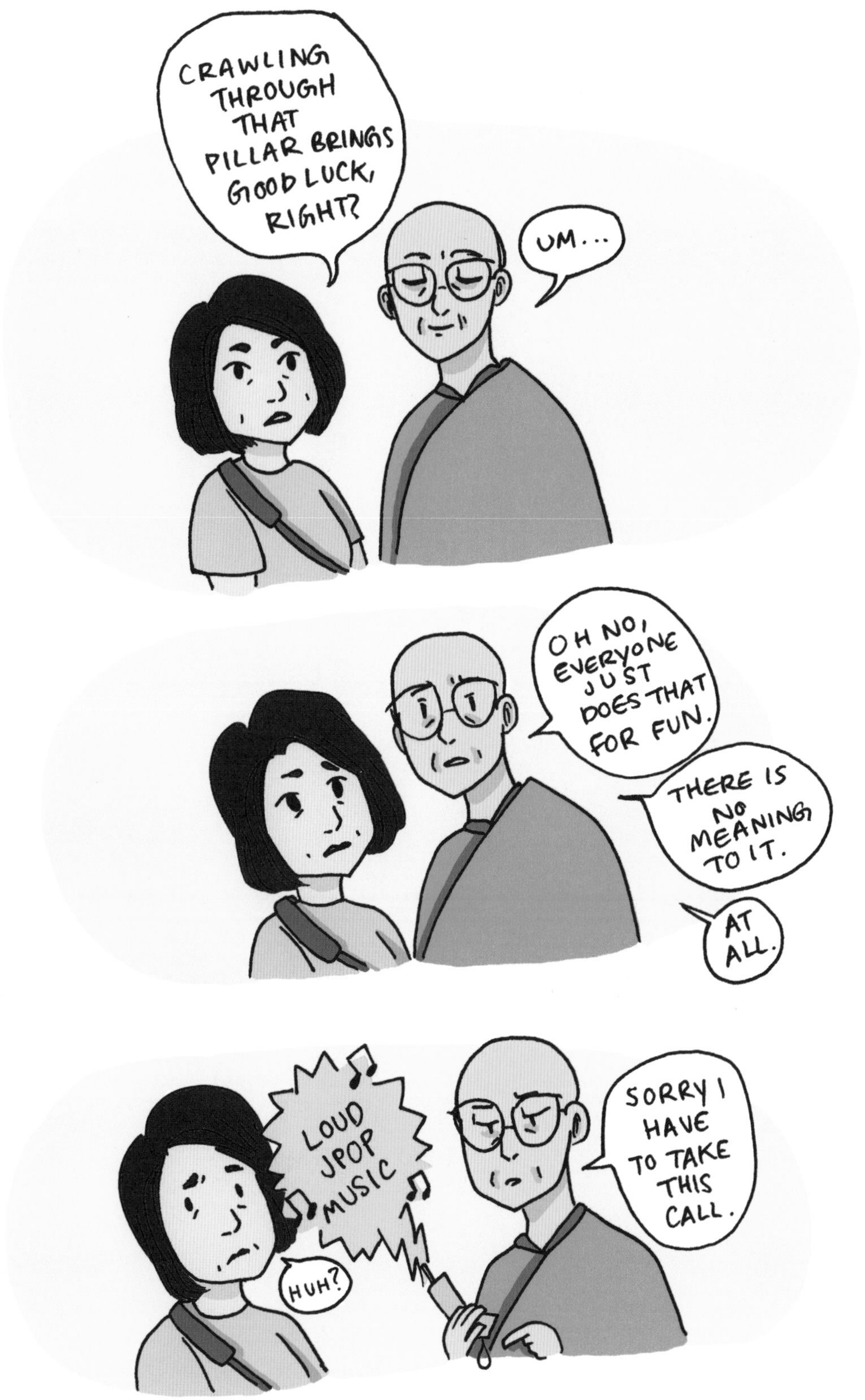

CRAWLING THROUGH THAT PILLAR BRINGS GOOD LUCK, RIGHT?
UM...
OH NO, EVERYONE JUST DOES THAT FOR FUN.
THERE IS NO MEANING TO IT.
AT ALL.
LOUD JPOP MUSIC
SORRY I HAVE TO TAKE THIS CALL.
HUH?

THESE GUYS ARE NATIONAL TREASURES, PROTECTED
BY THE GOVERNMENT. THEY ARE SPOILED ROTTEN
— EVERYONE WANTS TO FEED THEM!

THE DEER IN NARA

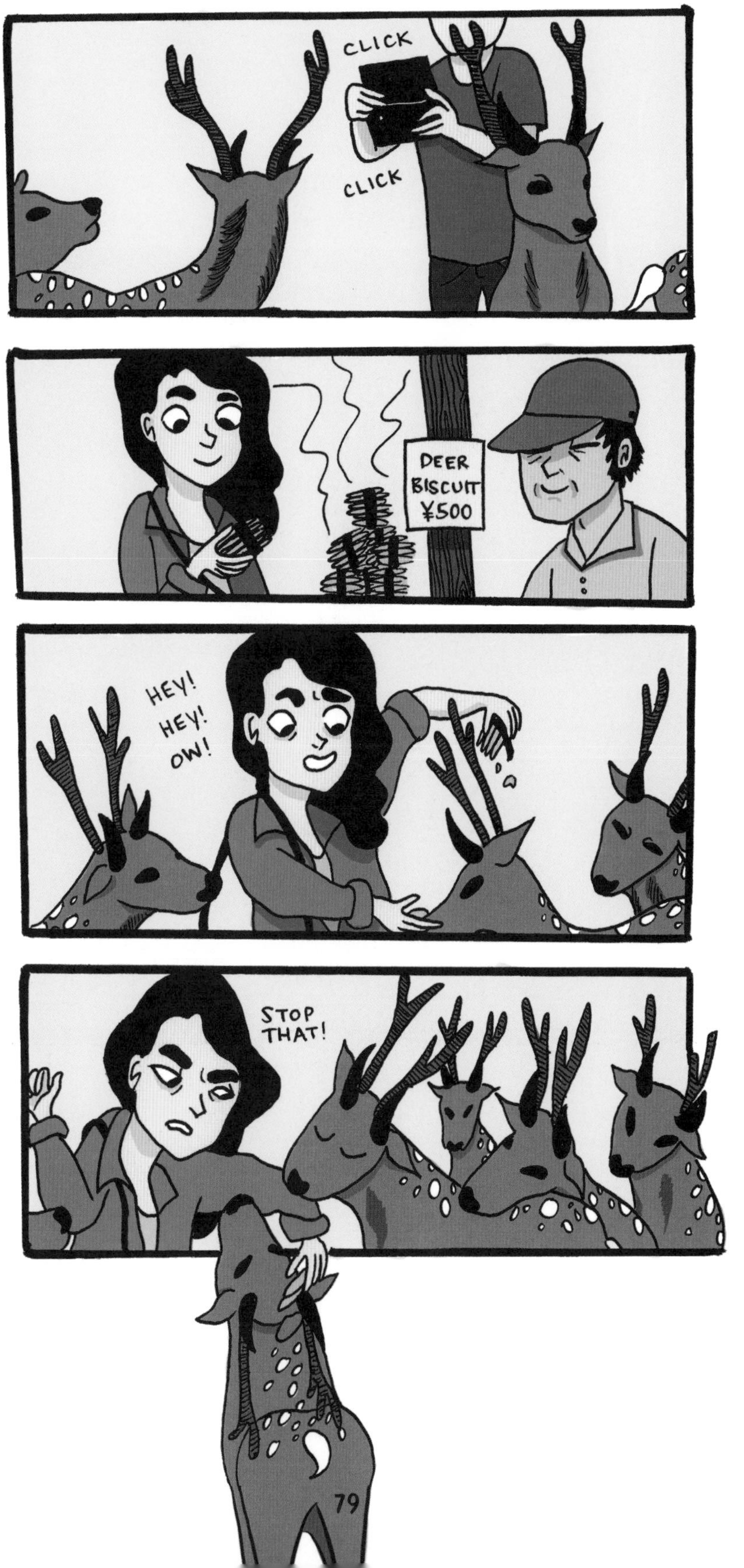

CLICK
CLICK
DEER BISCUIT ¥500
HEY! HEY! OW!
STOP THAT!

THE DAIBUTSU AT TODAIJI STANDS — OR SHOULD
I SAY SITS — 15 METERS (49 FEET) HIGH.

A DIALOGUE WITH DAIBUTSU

↑ AKA REALLY BIG BUDDHA

My favorite tourists

(WHILE IN KYOTO)

① LOVELY AUSTRALIANS I TALKED TO IN A STARBUCKS!

THEY WERE JUST A BIT OLDER THAN ME, PROBABLY HIGH SCHOOL SENIORS OR COLLEGE FRESHMEN.

THEY ALL WERE FRIENDS JUST VISITING JAPAN! WHEN I'M OLDER, I PLAN TO DO THIS...

② ATTRACTIVE, ARTISTIC-LOOKING YOUNG FOREIGNERS (I say this b/c they were not conversing in English) COUPLE

Babe lets blow dis taco joint

Probably what they were saying

He had silvery hair!

THEY WERE NOT AFRAID OF DISPLAYING THEIR AFFECTION. I LIKED GLARING AT THEM.

AS A FRIEND ONCE PUT IT, MAYBE "I JUST HATE BEAUTIFUL YOUNG PEOPLE"

③ THIS OLD LADY ON THE ESCALATOR. I ONLY EVER SAW THE BACK OF HER HEAD.

Blonde mohawk

Chain earring

"Unleash pain Peaceful World"

UNLEASH PAIN PEACEFUL WORLD

SHE WAS JAPANESE, AND HAD THE SWEETEST, PUREST VOICE. IT WAS A LITTLE WORN OUT FROM AGE.

④ TOTALLY RANDOM GROUP OF SMOKING HOT FRENCH GUYS ON THE BUS - THEY WOULDN'T SHUT UP EVER!

I'm going to stare at your butts the whole ride

Oui oui je suis beau croissant merde

Nous irons au «Kiyomizu?» Bla bla bla

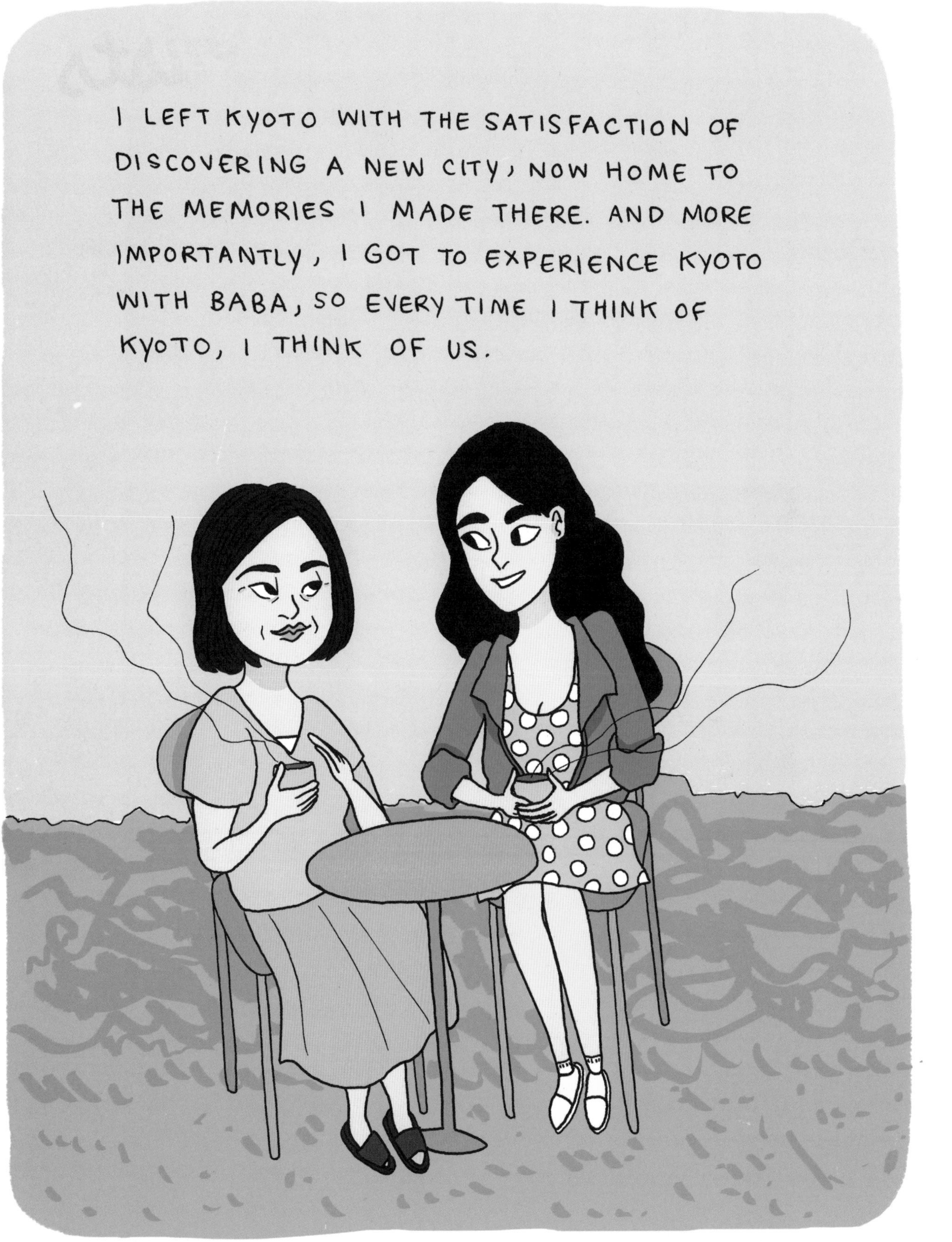
I LEFT KYOTO WITH THE SATISFACTION OF DISCOVERING A NEW CITY, NOW HOME TO THE MEMORIES I MADE THERE. AND MORE IMPORTANTLY, I GOT TO EXPERIENCE KYOTO WITH BABA, SO EVERY TIME I THINK OF KYOTO, I THINK OF US.

THE PROBLEM WITH JAPANESE BOYS

WHEN WE GOT BACK TO KASHIWA,
IT WAS TIME FOR MATSURI...

THIS IS PROBABLY NOT THE KIND OF SNACK YOU'D EXPECT TO SEE A SMALL CHILD HAPPILY EATING.

柏まつり

KASHIWA   MA - TSU - RI !

↑ WATAME

MASKS

THE KASHIWA MATSURI IS 2 DAYS LONG AND ATTRACTS AROUND 60 THOUSAND.

THESE ARE THE SORTS OF THINGS YOU'LL FIND AT EVERY MATSURI:

TO GET ONE, YOU HAVE TO TAKE A STRIP OF PAPER TIED TO A FISH HOOK AND GET THE FISH HOOK THRU THE YOYO'S HANDLE. IF THE PAPER GETS WET THE HOOK WILL FALL

YoYo Balloons
THESE ARE MY FAVORITE THINGS. I ALWAYS MAKE SURE TO GET ONE.

Fish in bags
I HATE THIS GAME SO I DON'T PLAY IT. YOU HAVE TO PICK UP A FISH WITH THIS NET THAT'S MADE OF PAPER AND IT ALWAYS BREAKS.

GRUNTING GUYS CARRYING THIS → DOWN THE STREET

I didn't get to see this up-close

YAKISOBA

OKONOMIYAKI

OK THE SHRINE IS TOO BIG BUT YOU GET THE PICTURE

TAKO

YAKITORI

IKA

SAKANA

KAKIGORI

THEY ALSO HAVE LITTLE LOTTERIES AND YOU PAY LIKE ¥500 AND PULL OUT A NUMBER THAT DETERMINES WHAT KIND OF PRIZE YOU WIN.

LITERALLY WINS THE BIGGEST PRIZE EVERY TIME

I SEE HOW IT IS ...

2 PACK OF MAGNETS

CONTRARY TO HOW IT LOOKS, THEY'RE NOT DANCING
IN THEIR STOCKING FEET. THOSE SOCKS (TABI) DO
HAVE SOLES.

THE BEST AND WORST PART IN THE ART BALLET SEGMENT WAS THEM DANCING TO LADY GAGA'S "LOVEGAME" FOR THEIR FINALE.

BUT MY FAVORITE PART OF MATSURI WAS THE **DANCERS!!!**

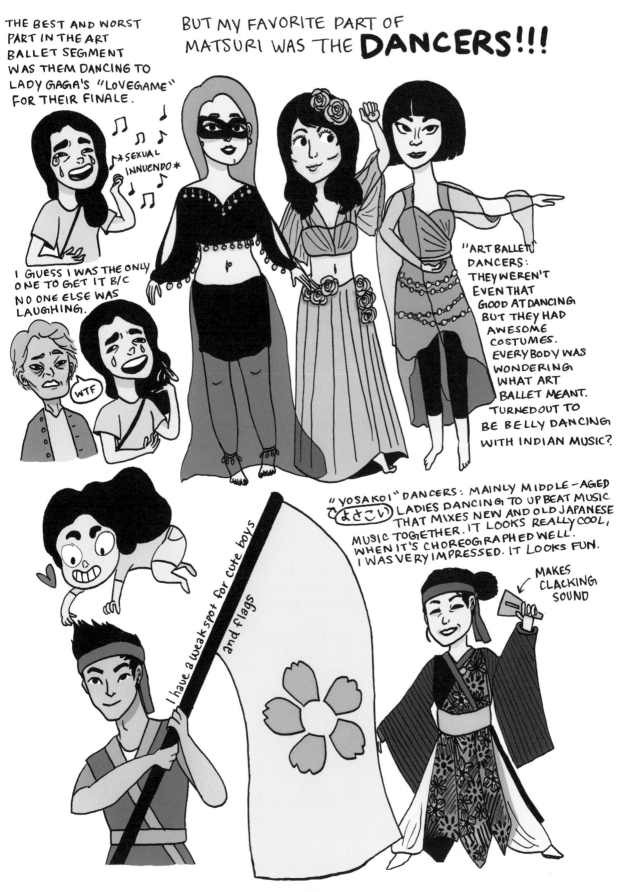

♪*SEXUAL INNUENDO*♪

I GUESS I WAS THE ONLY ONE TO GET IT B/C NO ONE ELSE WAS LAUGHING.

WTF

"ART BALLET" DANCERS: THEY WEREN'T EVEN THAT GOOD AT DANCING BUT THEY HAD AWESOME COSTUMES. EVERYBODY WAS WONDERING WHAT ART BALLET MEANT. TURNED OUT TO BE BELLY DANCING WITH INDIAN MUSIC?

"YOSAKOI" DANCERS: MAINLY MIDDLE-AGED
よさこい LADIES DANCING TO UPBEAT MUSIC THAT MIXES NEW AND OLD JAPANESE MUSIC TOGETHER. IT LOOKS REALLY COOL, WHEN IT'S CHOREOGRAPHED WELL. I WAS VERY IMPRESSED. IT LOOKS FUN.

I have a weak spot for cute boys and flags

MAKES CLACKING SOUND

WHAT'S THE POINT OF MATSURI, ANYWAY?

THERE WAS, HOWEVER, ONE OTHER FESTIVAL I ATTENDED WHERE I DID KNOW ITS CONTEXT. THE OBON FESTIVAL IS ABOUT HONORING THE FAMILY'S ANCESTORS. I WENT TO GO SEE THE DANCE THAT'S CUSTOMARY TO THE FESTIVAL.

I WISH I COULD HAVE DONNED MY OWN
KIMONO AND JOINED THEM.

IMAGINE IT. A HOT SUMMER AFTERNOON. THE SUN BEATS DOWN RELENTLESSLY ON YOU. YOU'RE ON A BLAZING CITY SIDEWALK WITHOUT ANY SHADE. YOU'RE SWEATING EVERYWHERE AND IT'S GROSS. YOUR THROAT IS PARCHED. AND THEN YOU SPOT THIS IN THE DISTANCE:

CHOOSE WHAT YOU WANT BY PUSHING THE BLACK BUTTON

PAY WITH CASH, COIN OR... SOMETIMES WITH A CARD TOO

RETRIEVE

ANGELS SING IN THE DISTANCE
IN JAPAN, YOU CAN ALWAYS COUNT ON FINDING A VENDING MACHINE SOMEWHERE — BECAUSE THEY'RE PRACTICALLY EVERYWHERE. I THINK PEOPLE EXPECT TO FIND MORE OF THE WEIRD*ONES THEY HEAR ABOUT, BUT MOST OF THEM JUST HAVE COLD DRINKS... TYPICALLY TEA, ICED COFFEE, JUICE, AND SPORTS DRINKS.

* I'VE HEARD ABOUT VENDING MACHINES THAT SELL UNDERWEAR

THE TOILET STRUGGLE CONTINUES AS I DISCOVER A SET OF BUTTONS ON THE HOUSE TOILET.

BZZT!

NATURALLY, I DECIDED TO DO SOME INVESTIGATING.

SPLASH

...

THE FAMILY ARRIVES

!!!

I CAN'T BELIEVE I'VE BEEN IN JAPAN FOR 6 WEEKS. TIME HAS FLOWN. AND TODAY MY FAMILY IS COMING!!!

MY FAMILY
They arrived yesterday

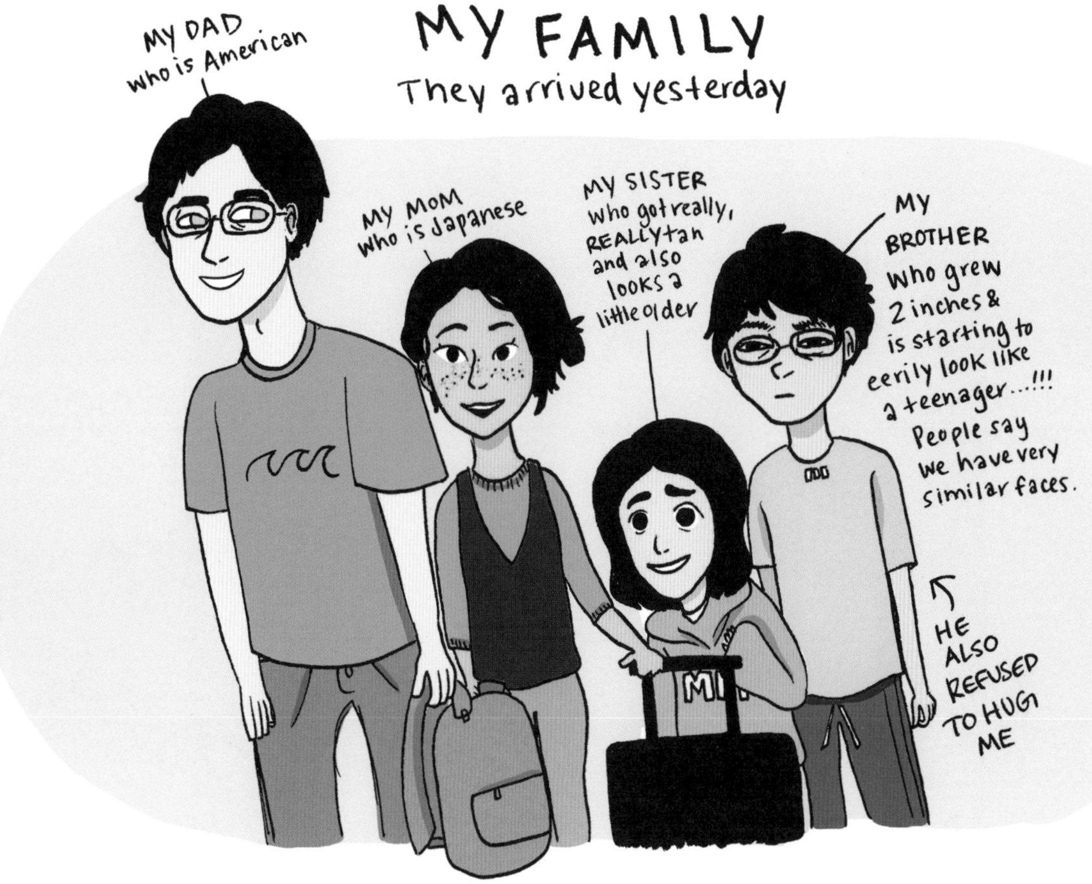
MY DAD who is American
MY MOM who is Japanese
MY SISTER who got really, REALLY tan and also looks a little older
MY BROTHER who grew 2 inches & is starting to eerily look like a teenager...!!! People say we have very similar faces.
HE ALSO REFUSED TO HUG ME

I DIDN'T REALLY MISS MY FAMILY UNTIL IT DAWNED ON ME THAT THEY WERE COMING AND I'D GET TO SEE THEM. SOMETHING THAT I HAVEN'T CONFESSED YET IS IT'S PRETTY LONELY HERE, AND I'M LOOKING FORWARD TO DOING THINGS IN JAPAN WITH THEM, AS A FAMILY.

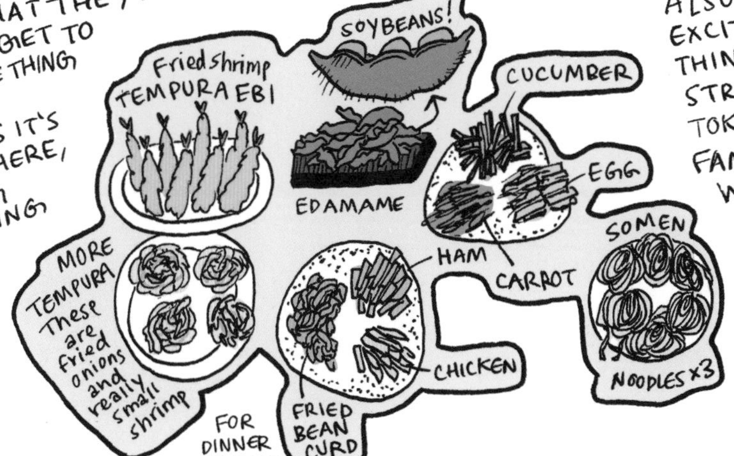
SOYBEANS!
Fried shrimp TEMPURA EBI
EDAMAME
CUCUMBER
EGG
CARROT
HAM
MORE TEMPURA These are fried onions and really small shrimp
CHICKEN
FRIED BEAN CURD
SOMEN
NOODLES x3

ALSO, IT'S VERY EXCITING TO THINK I'LL BE STROLLING AROUND TOKYO WITH MY FAMILY, JUST LIKE WHEN I WAS LITTLE!

FOR DINNER WE HAD **SOMEN**.

THIS IS HOW YOU EAT IT:

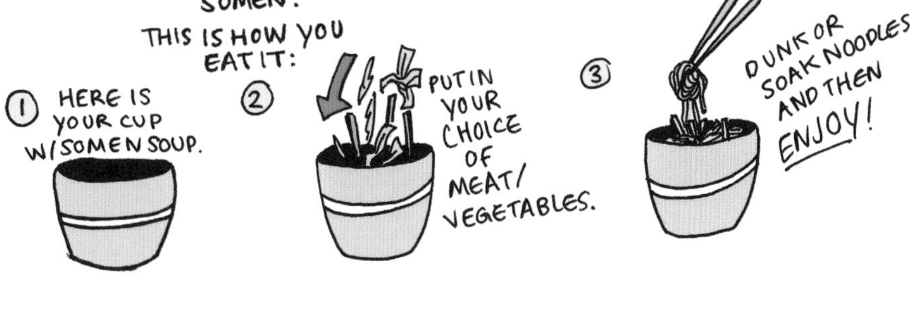
1 HERE IS YOUR CUP W/SOMEN SOUP.
2 PUT IN YOUR CHOICE OF MEAT/VEGETABLES.
3 DUNK OR SOAK NOODLES AND THEN ENJOY!

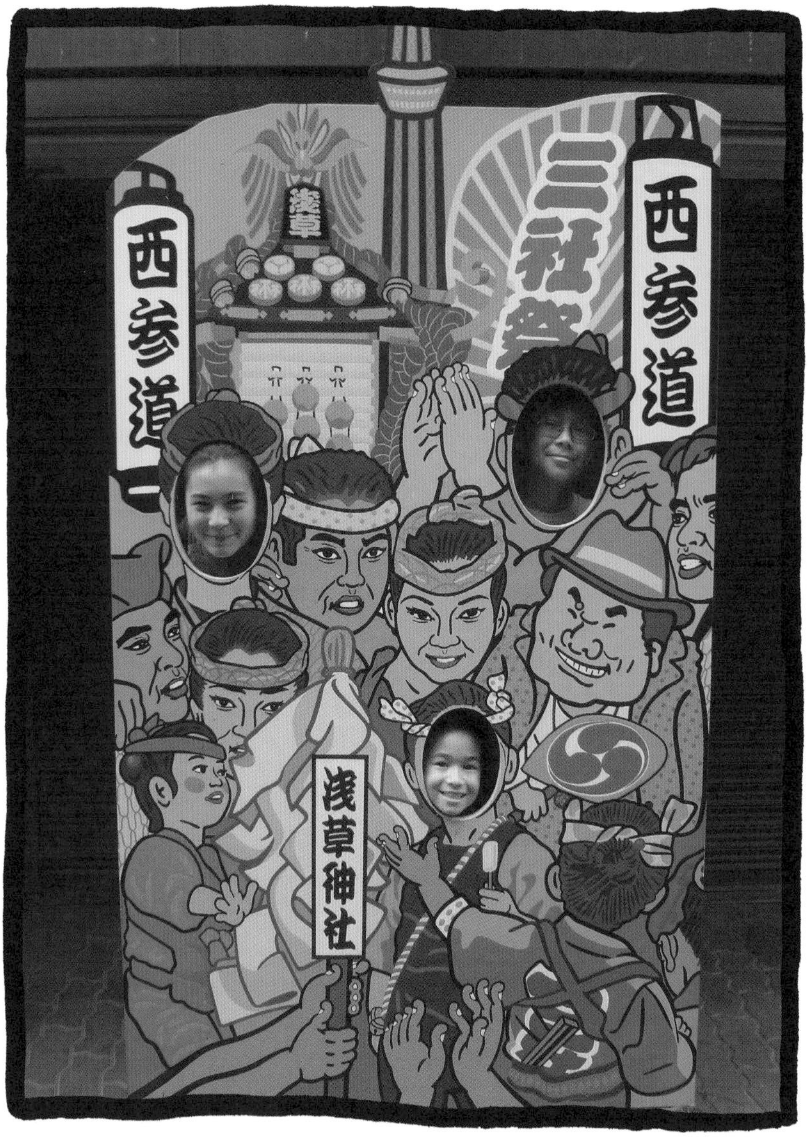
西参道
浅草
三社祭
西参道
浅草神社

TAKEN IN ASAKUSA.

IT'S TIME TO EXPLORE ...

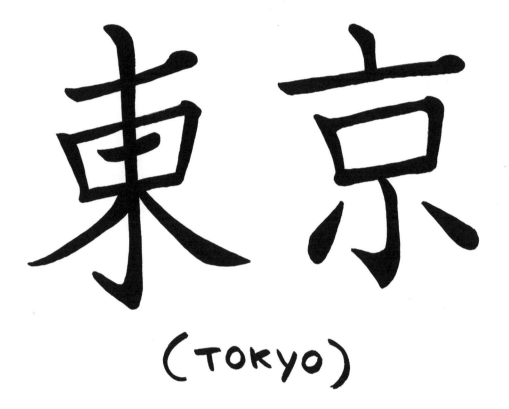

東京

(TOKYO)

I'M STANDING IN FRONT OF A SUSHI LOVER'S
DREAM. TSUKIJI HAS MORE KINDS OF FISH
THAN YOU CAN IMAGINE.

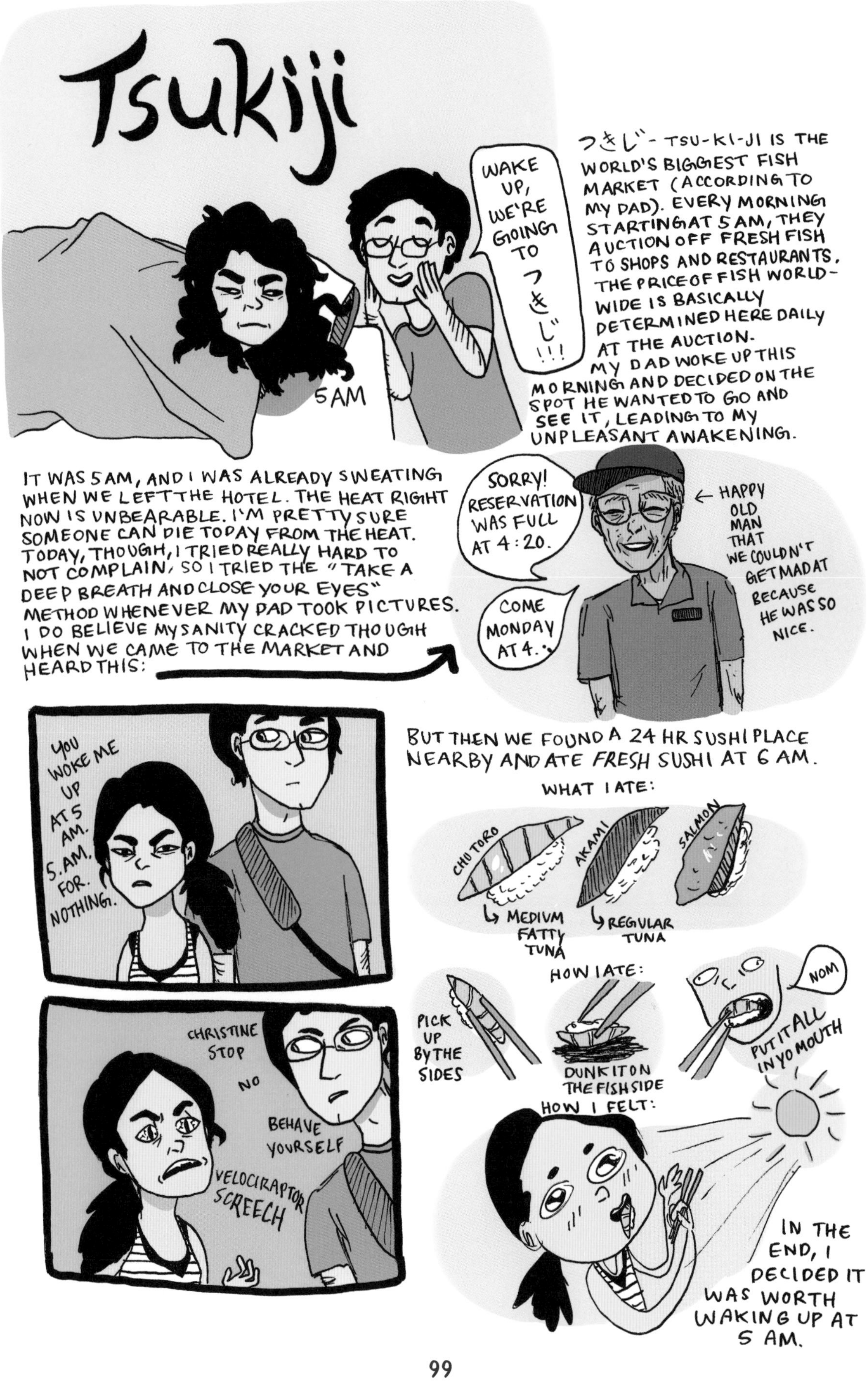
Tsukiji
WAKE UP, WE'RE GOING TO つきじ !!!
つきじ - TSU-KI-JI IS THE WORLD'S BIGGEST FISH MARKET (ACCORDING TO MY DAD). EVERY MORNING STARTING AT 5 AM, THEY AUCTION OFF FRESH FISH TO SHOPS AND RESTAURANTS. THE PRICE OF FISH WORLD-WIDE IS BASICALLY DETERMINED HERE DAILY AT THE AUCTION.
MY DAD WOKE UP THIS MORNING AND DECIDED ON THE SPOT HE WANTED TO GO AND SEE IT, LEADING TO MY UNPLEASANT AWAKENING.
5 AM
IT WAS 5 AM, AND I WAS ALREADY SWEATING WHEN WE LEFT THE HOTEL. THE HEAT RIGHT NOW IS UNBEARABLE. I'M PRETTY SURE SOMEONE CAN DIE TODAY FROM THE HEAT. TODAY, THOUGH, I TRIED REALLY HARD TO NOT COMPLAIN, SO I TRIED THE "TAKE A DEEP BREATH AND CLOSE YOUR EYES" METHOD WHENEVER MY DAD TOOK PICTURES. I DO BELIEVE MY SANITY CRACKED THOUGH WHEN WE CAME TO THE MARKET AND HEARD THIS:
SORRY! RESERVATION WAS FULL AT 4:20.
COME MONDAY AT 4.
← HAPPY OLD MAN THAT WE COULDN'T GET MAD AT BECAUSE HE WAS SO NICE.
YOU WOKE ME UP AT 5 AM. 5 AM. FOR NOTHING.
CHRISTINE STOP
NO
BEHAVE YOURSELF
VELOCIRAPTOR SCREECH
BUT THEN WE FOUND A 24 HR SUSHI PLACE NEARBY AND ATE FRESH SUSHI AT 6 AM.
WHAT I ATE:
CHU TORO
AKAMI
SALMON
MEDIUM FATTY TUNA
REGULAR TUNA
HOW I ATE:
PICK UP BY THE SIDES
DUNK IT ON THE FISH SIDE
NOM
PUT IT ALL IN YO MOUTH
HOW I FELT:
IN THE END, I DECIDED IT WAS WORTH WAKING UP AT 5 AM.

KAMINARIMON ...

... THAT MEANS "THUNDER GATE." THAT LANTERN WEIGHS ALMOST 1500 POUNDS.

ASAKUSA

I WENT TO ASAKUSA AND KAMINARIMON TWICE: FIRST WITH JUST MY DAD, THEN WITH MY ENTIRE FAMILY. KAMINARIMON IS A VERY FAMOUS GATE LEADING TO A TEMPLE AND BASICALLY EVERYONE STANDS IN FRONT OF IT AND TRIES TO TAKE A PICTURE. SINCE I JUST WENT TO KYOTO, I WAS NOT THAT IMPRESSED BY IT, EXCEPT FOR ITS *HUGE* LANTERN.

WE WALKED UP TO THE TEMPLE AND DID THE USUAL TOURIST-Y THINGS (THERE WERE A LOT OF TOURISTS) AND THEN WE LEFT TO FIND FOOD. ON OUR WAY TO THE RESTAURANT, WE RAN INTO THIS TOTALLY CRAZY LADY – SHE WOULD STOP AND TALK TO ANYTHING MOVING ON THE STREET. SHE WAS REALLY FRIENDLY, AND IT SEEMED LIKE SHE WAS JUST LOOKING OUT FOR EVERYONE.

SOBA

FOR LUNCH WE HAD ZARU SOBA AND TEMPURA

AND

WE SAT ON PILLOWS LIKE THIS

SOUP

TEMPURA

It was delicious

mister Donut

IN AMERICA, WE HAVE DUNKIN DONUTS AND KRISPY KREME. IN JAPAN, MISTER DONUT REIGNS OVER THE DONUT BUSINESS. THESE ARE THEIR 3 MOST COMMON DONUTS:

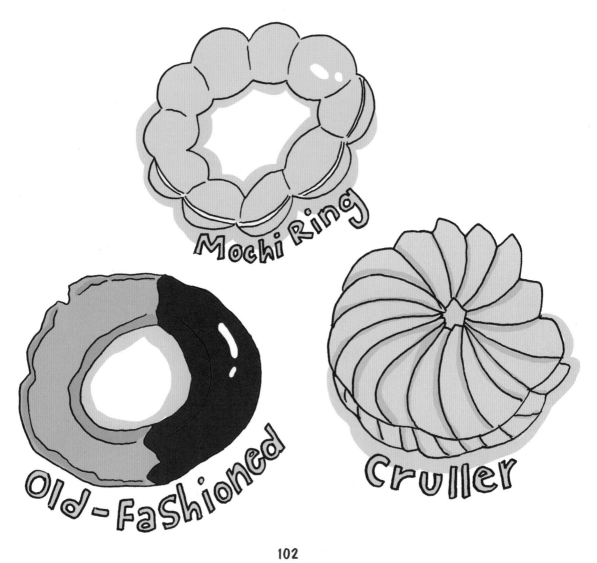

Mochi Ring

Old-Fashioned

Cruller

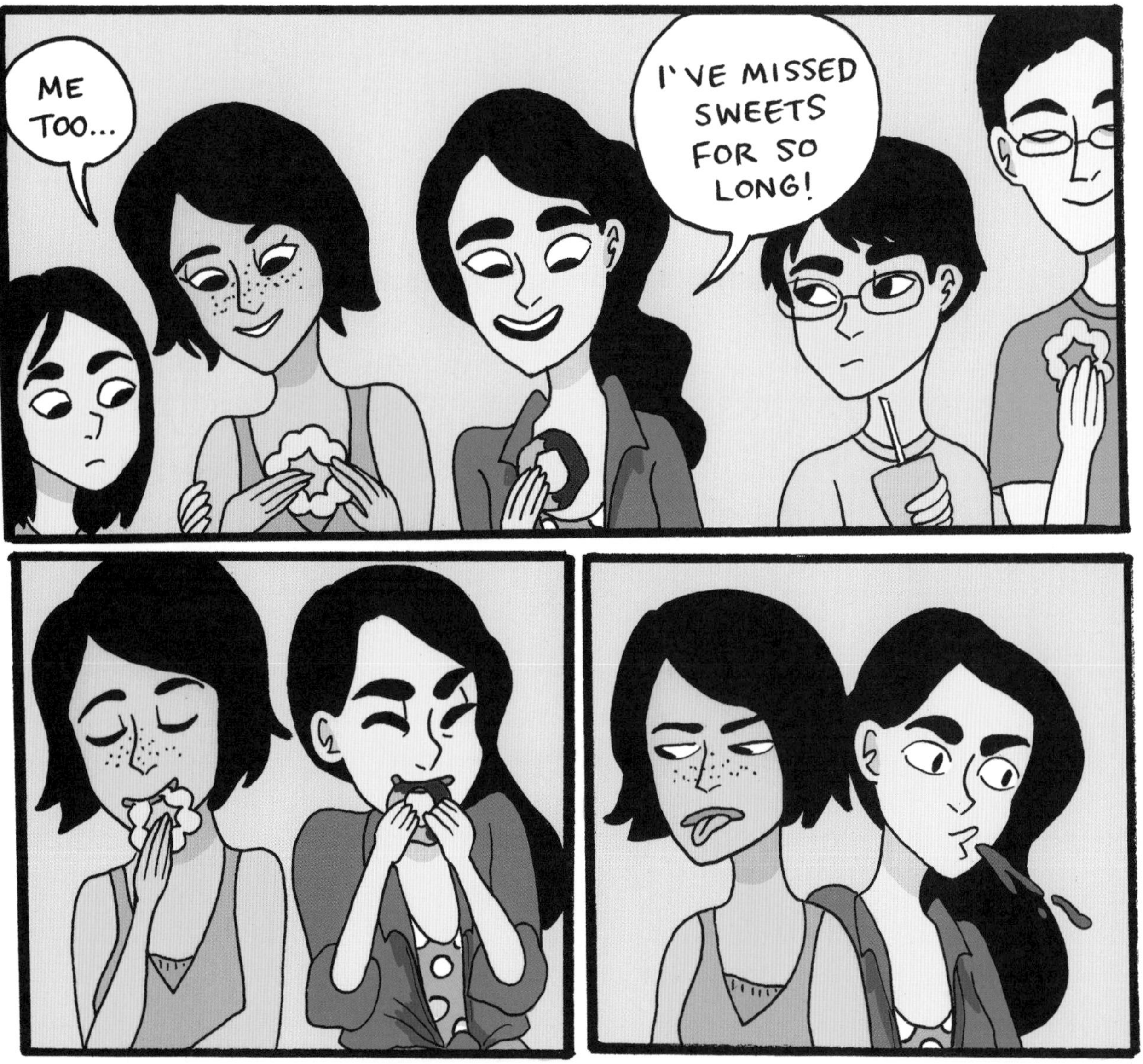
ME TOO...
I'VE MISSED SWEETS FOR SO LONG!

A NOTE TO ANY FOREIGNERS: JAPAN'S DEFINITION OF SWEET IS, WELL, NOT VERY SWEET. KEEP AN OPEN MIND AS YOU TRY THEIR SWEETS, SUCH AS MISTER DONUT DONUTS............. OR, IF YOU'RE MY MOM AND I, JUST FIND A KRISPY KREME SOMEWHERE.

THIS CANNOT BE AN EASY JOB...

Maidtown

✦ WENT TO ✦ AKIHABARA ✦

WEIRDLY, THIS PLACE HAS THE MOST "POP CULTURE" STUFF, BUT IT WAS MY LEAST FAVORITE PLACE TO VISIT. I JUST... I WASN'T REALLY KEEN ON THE WHOLE SUBMISSIVE ANIME DREAM GIRL THING THEY HAD GOING ON. I DON'T HAVE ANYTHING AGAINST ANYONE WHO LIKES ANIME/MANGA! BUT UH... UH.- I'M JUST NOT USED TO IT. IT CERTAINLY WAS INTERESTING THOUGH. ONE THING I DID NOT SEE ANYWHERE ELSE WERE THE "MAIDS" ON THE SIDEWALKS PROMOTING THEIR MAID CAFÉS! THEY WERE FUN TO SEE, BUT I FELT SO BAD BECAUSE IT WAS SO HOT AND A LOT OF PEOPLE JUST WALKED PAST THEM (AS DO MOST PEOPLE WITH ANYONE HANDING OUT ANYTHING).

OK AS YOU CAN TELL I CAN'T DRAW ANIME/ MANGA VERY WELL...

HM.

HA HA HA

COME

HIIIII

PLEASE JUST COME TO THE DAMN CAFÉ

HEE HEE

HIII

HI!

105

Rebels (sic)

ON SUNDAYS AT YOYOGI PARK, YOU MIGHT HAPPEN TO STUMBLE UPON A GROUP OF SHIRTLESS MIDDLE-AGED MEN WITH MAGNIFICENT GREASED HAIR DANCING TO OLD-TIMEY ROCK AND ROLL. THESE ARE THE ROCKABILLIES, AND THEY'VE BEEN DANCING HERE AT YOYOGI SINCE MY FATHER FIRST CAME AS A STUDENT...

MY QUEEN

HE DIDN'T LOOK LIKE THE REST OF THEM, BUT HE WAS IN THEIR GROUP. THEIR WIVES AND KIDS CAME TO WATCH, AND HE AND ONE OF THEIR DAUGHTERS WENT TO THE VENDING MACHINE SO HE COULD BUY HER AN APPLE JUICE.

THE LEADER

HE DOESN'T REALLY DANCE, BUT HE HANDLES THE MUSIC.

AIR GUITAR

SEARCH YOUTUBE FOR "LEBELS HARAJUKU" TO
SEE THEM IN ACTION.

I DON'T EVEN WANT TO KNOW WHAT'S INSIDE.

oh God

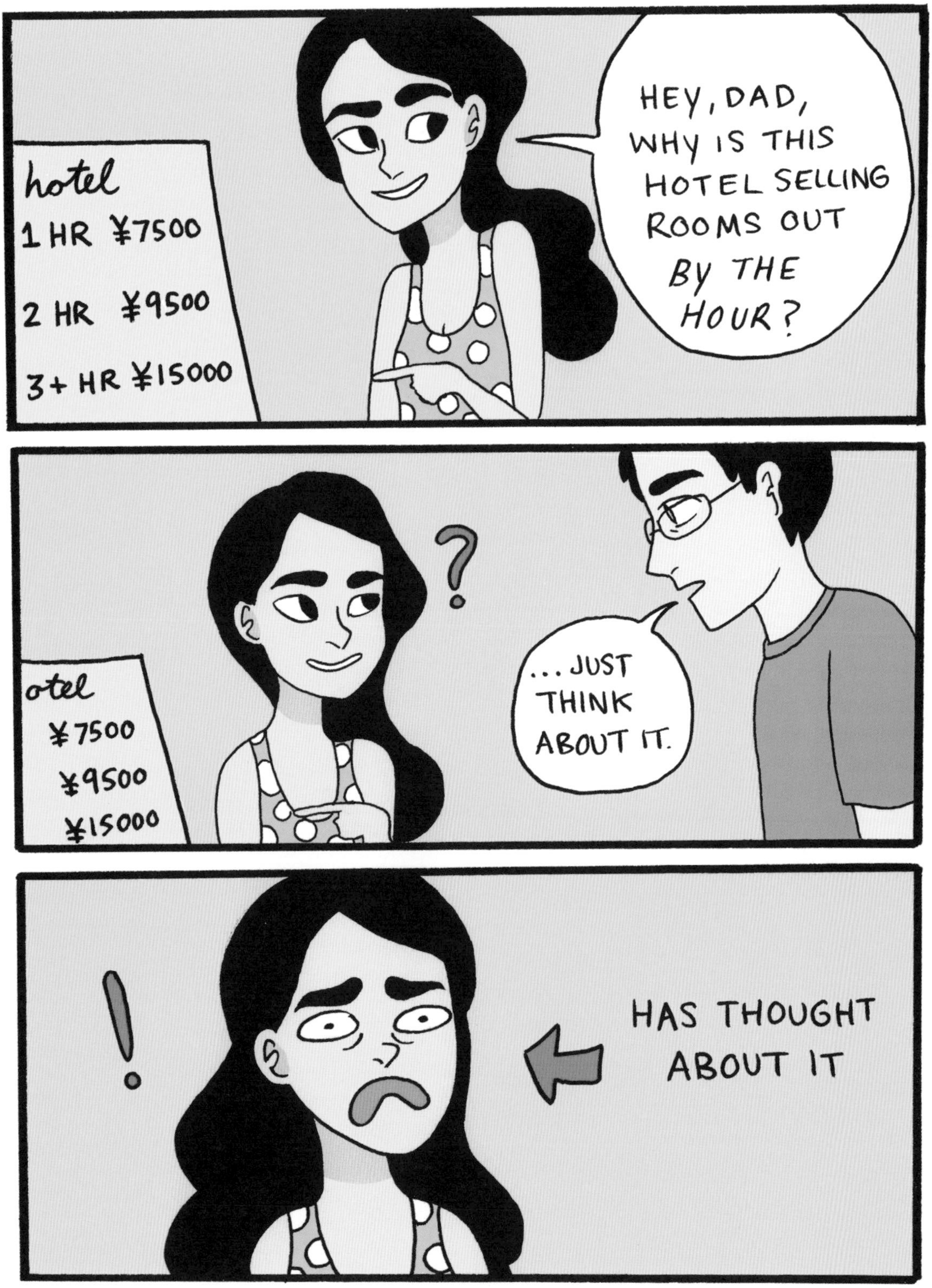

hotel
1 HR ¥7500
2 HR ¥9500
3+ HR ¥15000
HEY, DAD, WHY IS THIS HOTEL SELLING ROOMS OUT BY THE HOUR?
otel
¥7500
¥9500
¥15000
?
... JUST THINK ABOUT IT.
!
HAS THOUGHT ABOUT IT

WHAT IS...

KAITEN SUSHI,

YOU ASK?

It's a sushi place where plates of sushi are put on a rotating conveyor belt for customers to pick from.

MY FAMILY AND I STOPPED AT ONE IN HARAJUKU

THE COLOR OF THE PLATE INDICATES THE PRICE

THERE WERE FIVE OF US, REMEMBER!!!

teenagers...?

WHILE I'VE BEEN HERE, I KEEP LOOKING AROUND FOR ANY TEENAGERS MY AGE, WHICH BROUGHT ME TO A DISCOVERY ABOUT JAPANESE TEENAGE GIRLS:

THEY EITHER LOOK TOO young FOR THEIR AGE OR OLD ENOUGH TO BE OUT OF SCHOOL. THERE IS NO IN BETWEEN. MAYBE I'M THE IN BETWEEN...

(I THINK MAKE-UP HAS A LARGE ROLE IN THIS.)

IF ONLY I LOOKED THAT GOOD GOING
TO SCHOOL...

IF THERE IS ANY RITE OF PASSAGE
TO VISITING JAPAN, IT'S PROBABLY
TO HAVE A BOWL OF
RAMEN.

I CANNOT BELIEVE I HAVE NOT TALKED ABOUT RAMEN YET.

I'VE MENTIONED IT, PROBABLY, BUT HAVE I GIVEN IT ITS OWN PAGE YET? BECAUSE IT NEEDS ONE. I LOVE RAMEN. I EVEN LOVE TO DRAW IT.

NORI (SEAWEED)

BAMBOO

SOFT BOILED EGG

THIS IS WHAT A TYPICAL RAMEN HAS.

PORK

GREEN ONION

I THINK RAMEN IS BEAUTIFUL BECAUSE IT IS SO COMMON. YOU CAN FIND DECENT RAMEN ANYWHERE IN JAPAN. EVERYBODY EATS IT. I SEE CONSTRUCTION WORKERS EATING IT DURING THEIR LUNCH BREAK, THEN I SEE MOVIE STARS IN PHOTOS EATING — YOU GUESSED IT, RAMEN.

HACHIKO

(AKA GET READY TO CRY YOUR EYES OUT)

THIS IS **HACHIKO.** WELL, IT'S REALLY A STATUE OF HIM. ↳

YOU CAN FIND HIS STATUE AT SHIBUYA STATION. YOU MIGHT BE WONDERING WHY THERE EVEN IS A STATUE DEDICATED TO A DOG. THIS IS WHY:

THIS IS HACHIKO'S OWNER, HIDESABURŌ UENO, WHO COMMUTED TO WORK FROM SHIBUYA STATION.

EVERY DAY, HACHIKO WOULD WAIT IN FRONT OF SHIBUYA STATION FOR HIS OWNER TO RETURN FROM WORK. ONE DAY, UENO DID NOT RETURN. HE HAD SUFFERED A STROKE AND PASSED AWAY.

BUT HACHIKO CONTINUED TO COME TO THE STATION EACH AND EVERY DAY UNTIL HIS OWN DEATH 9 YEARS LATER. HE WON JAPAN'S HEART AND SO THEY MADE THIS STATUE IN HIS HONOR.

ME, CIRCA EARLY 2000'S WITH HACHIKO!

LOOK HOW STYLISH I WAS

EVERYBODY LOVES A CANINE HERO.

RETURNING HERE GIVES ME NO BETTER FEELING ON THIS EARTH. SURE, IT'S NO FIVE STAR RESTAURANT — IT'S EVEN BETTER.

Homework's

THIS PLACE IS HOME TO SOME OF MY MOST VIVID MEMORIES OF LIVING IN TOKYO WHEN I WAS LITTLE. HOMEWORK'S IS A SMALL RESTAURANT THAT SERVES AMERICAN STYLE FOOD - BURGERS, SHAKES, FRIES, ETC. I HAD BEEN EATING THERE SINCE I WAS A CHILD. MY SIGNATURE MEAL CONSISTED OF A TUNA SANDWICH, FRENCH FRIES, AND A CHOCOLATE MILKSHAKE I SHARED WITH MY DAD.

2000:

2013:

I NOTICED THIS FAMILY AS I WAS LEAVING. SOME THINGS NEVER CHANGE.

heading HOME

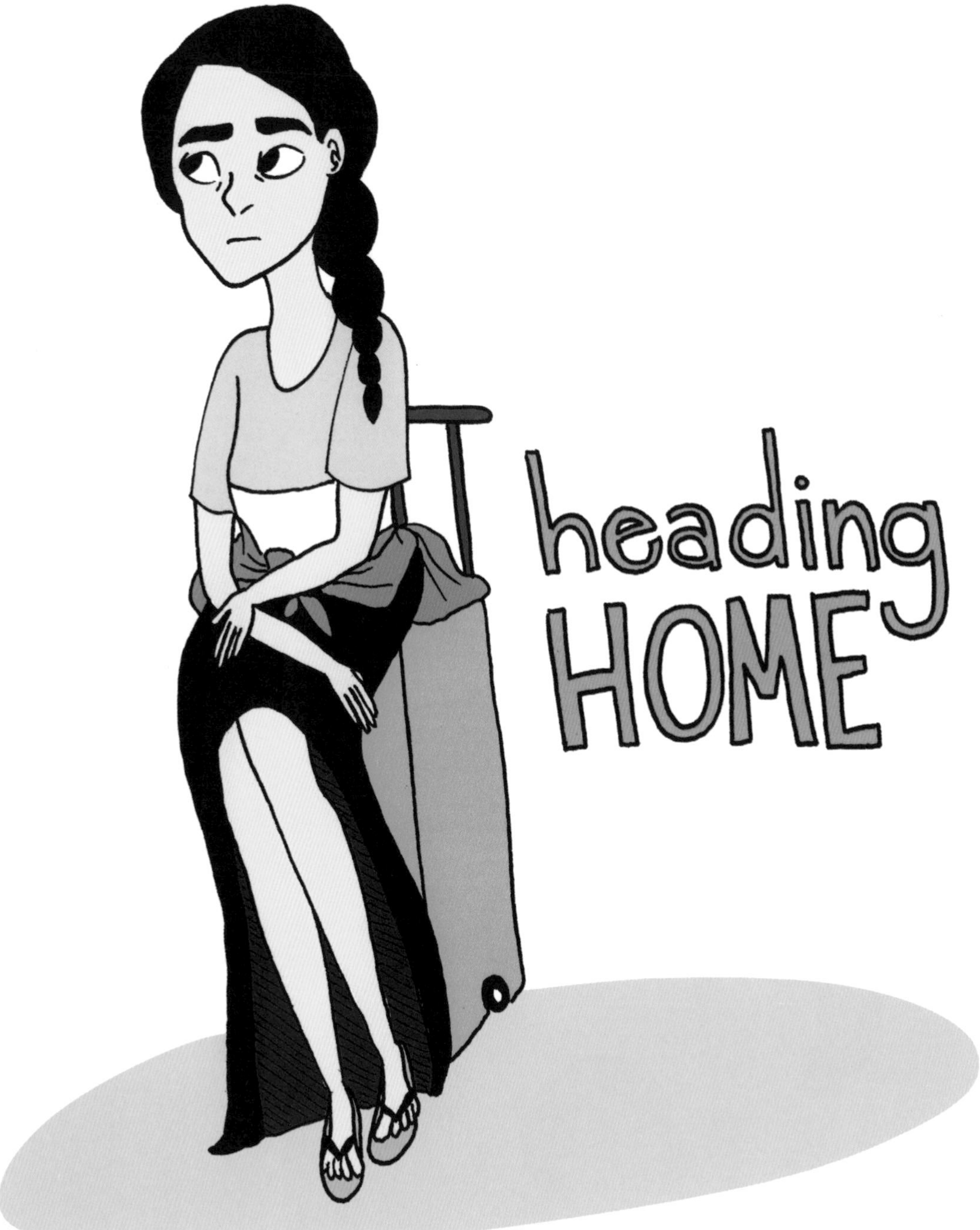

THIS IS IT.

THE BRUTAL REALIZATION HIT ME ONLY THE DAY BEFORE: I HAVE TO GO HOME.

BLACK ROOTS

BROWN HAIR

A SHIRT

SWATCH

SOME ARTSY FARTSY PURSE

SHAPELESS SKIRT

I DREW MYSELF THE DAY I LEFT AMERICA. THE DIFFERENCE IN HOW I DREW MYSELF THERE AND HERE IS... SHOCKING?

FLIP FLOPS BECAUSE I DON'T CARE

I FEEL LIKE A DIFFERENT PERSON. I FEEL MORE CONFIDENT. EVEN A LITTLE SMARTER.

DID I CRY?

YES. AS USUAL. I'VE NEVER PUT MUCH THOUGHT INTO WHY THOUGH. JUST SAYING I'M SAD DOESN'T EXPLAIN IT.
I'M SAD, BUT NOT BECAUSE I DON'T WANT TO LEAVE. I WILL MISS IT, BUT I ALSO WANT TO GO HOME. WHAT WAS MOST PAINFUL WAS WHEN THE TRAIN DOORS CLOSED, AND BABA WAS STANDING OUTSIDE. AND ALSO, THE SCENERY OUTSIDE THE WINDOW, OLD HOUSE ROOFTOPS AND RICE FIELDS AND EVERYTHING SO VIVID WITH COLOR AND I WAS PASSING BY ALL OF IT FOR THE LAST TIME, I FELT THIS BIG LUMP IN MY THROAT AND A SWELL IN MY CHEST LIKE YOU GET WHEN SOME INDESCRIBABLE EMOTION GRABS AHOLD OF YOU. AND THOSE TWO THINGS, MY GRANDMA AND THE WINDOW, MADE ME CRY.

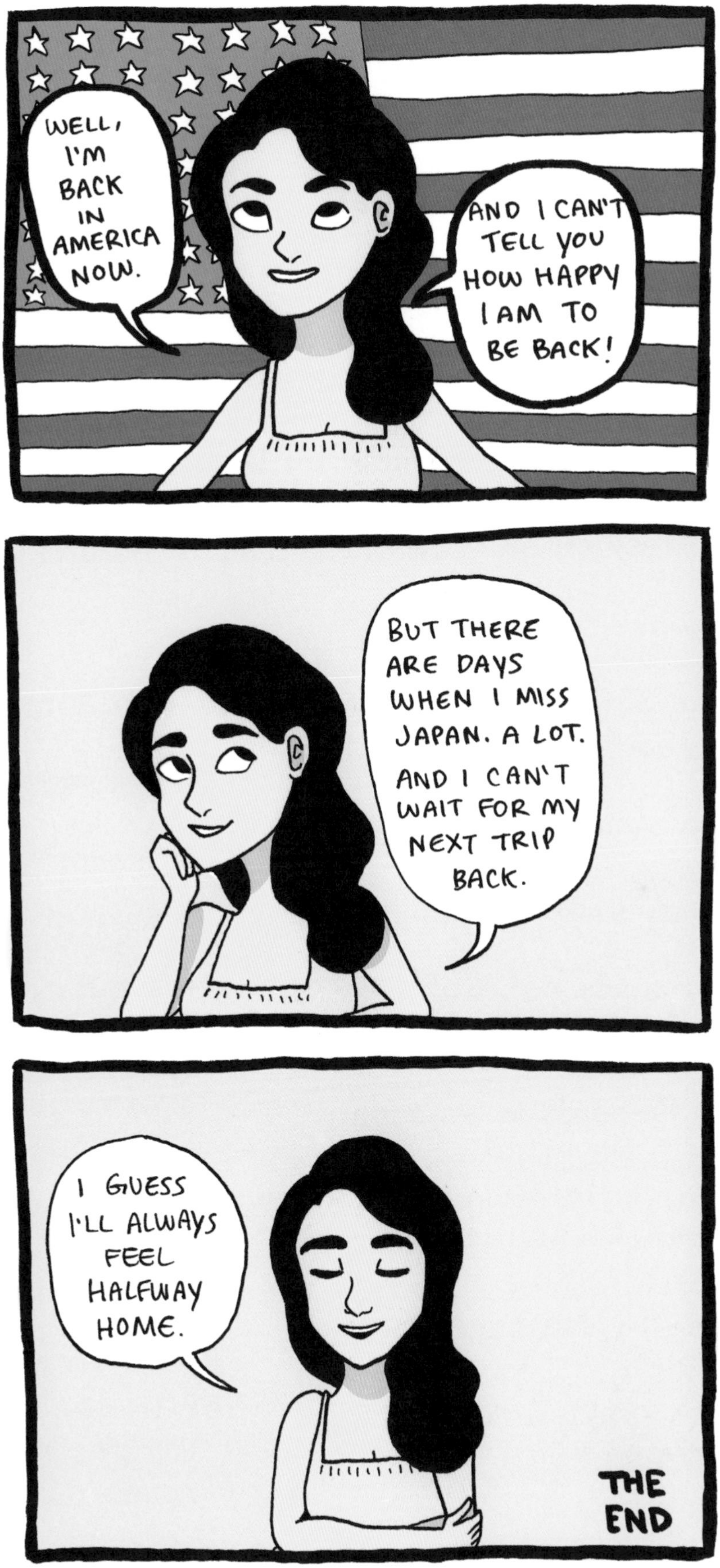
WELL, I'M BACK IN AMERICA NOW.
AND I CAN'T TELL YOU HOW HAPPY I AM TO BE BACK!
BUT THERE ARE DAYS WHEN I MISS JAPAN. A LOT. AND I CAN'T WAIT FOR MY NEXT TRIP BACK.
I GUESS I'LL ALWAYS FEEL HALFWAY HOME.
THE END

♡ THINGS I LOVE ABOUT JAPAN ♡

waiting for the light to turn green at Shibuya crossing in the early evening.

Ramen. Enough said.

People watching on the Yamanote line.

The Wind-Up Bird Chronicle by Haruki Murakami.

Street fashion on Takeshita-dori in Harajuku.

Mosburger.

Looking down at the maze of streets that is Tokyo from the top of Skytree.

Totoro by Hayao Miyazaki.

Stacking empty plates at kaiten-zushi.

The Japanese habit of apologizing for everything – something I recognize in myself.

Tower Records in Shibuya.

Lunch at Homeworks in Hiroo, where we used to go when I was little.

Botchan by Natsume Soseki.

Buying fresh sashimi for dinner in the late afternoon with Baba.

ACKNOWLEDGMENTS

I'd like to thank the following people who in one way or another helped me to write this book.

A very special thanks to Terri Jadick, my editor at Tuttle, for taking a chance on a teenage author.

Thanks to Makoto Ozaki, my father's friend and an awesome photographer who provided us with some pictures for the book. Visit his website at www.hellomakoto.com.

To my mother Ayumi, who always knew what to say to keep me focused on finishing this book.

To Baba and JiJi, my Japanese grandparents, who let me stay with them all summer and made my experience in Japan possible. I especially want to give my love to Baba, for showing me around Tokyo and Kyoto, for her delicious meals, and for keeping me company so I never felt alone.

To the Terajima family, aka my aunt Megu, uncle Ryota, and two precious cousins Taiga and Karen, who made my stay fun and helped me feel at home in Kashiwa.

To BlaBla and Pepaw, my American grandparents, for their unlimited love and support.

To my brother Stefan and sister Zoe, who drive me crazy most of the time, but whom I love nonetheless.

To all of my teachers. I'm quiet in class, but I hope my voice sings clear to you in this book.

To my friends and peers. Over the years you have been telling me to do something with my artistic passion... so here it is!

I sent an advance copy of the book to a number of authors and comic artists I respect and admire. I was overwhelmed by the response I received. Their feedback and suggestions were invaluable and helped me to make a better book. To them, arigato gozaimasu!

Finally, thanks to the person who sat next to me one afternoon and convinced me to fly to Japan and write this book in the first place, who urged me to seek out exciting experiences during my trip, who offered suggestions and encouragement when I got stuck, who tirelessly corrected my grammar and edited each and every page, and who constantly assured me that I could finish this book when I felt like I couldn't. He also happens to be my father. Thanks dad.

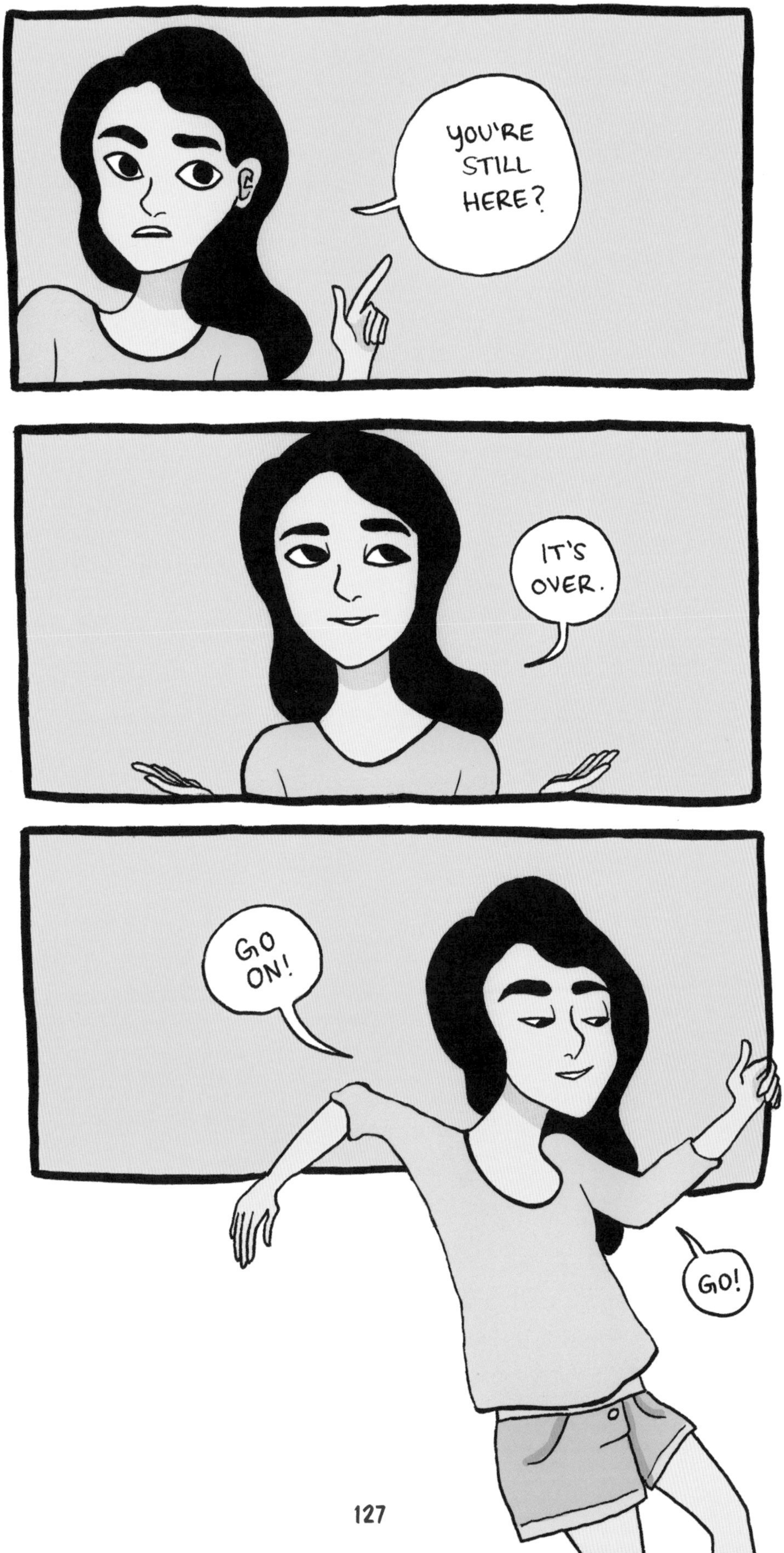
YOU'RE STILL HERE?
IT'S OVER.
GO ON!
GO!

"Books to Span the East and West"

Tuttle Publishing was founded in 1832 in the small New England town of Rutland, Vermont [USA]. Our core values remain as strong today as they were then—to publish best-in-class books which bring people together one page at a time. In 1948, we established a publishing office in Japan—and Tuttle is now a leader in publishing English-language books about the arts, languages and cultures of Asia. The world has become a much smaller place today and Asia's economic and cultural influence has grown. Yet the need for meaningful dialogue and information about this diverse region has never been greater. Over the past seven decades, Tuttle has published thousands of books on subjects ranging from martial arts and paper crafts to language learning and literature—and our talented authors, illustrators, designers and photographers have won many prestigious awards. We welcome you to explore the wealth of information available on Asia at www.tuttlepublishing.com.

Published by Tuttle Publishing, an imprint of Periplus Editions (HK) Ltd.

www.tuttlepublishing.com

Copyright @ 2016 by Christine Mari Inzer

Library of Congress Control Number: 2016940613

ISBN 978-4-8053-1396-1

First edition
24 23 22 21   8 7 6 5
Printed in China   2111EP

Distributed by

North America, Latin America & Europe
Tuttle Publishing
364 Innovation Drive
North Clarendon,
VT 05759-9436 U.S.A.
Tel: (802) 773-8930
Fax: (802) 773-6993
info@tuttlepublishing.com
www.tuttlepublishing.com

Japan
Tuttle Publishing
Yaekari Building, 3rd Floor
5-4-12 Osaki, Shinagawa-ku
Tokyo 141 0032
Tel: (81) 3 5437-0171
Fax: (81) 3 5437-0755
sales@tuttle.co.jp
www.tuttle.co.jp

Asia Pacific
Berkeley Books Pte. Ltd.
3 Kallang Sector #04-01
Singapore 349278
Tel: (65) 6741-2178
Fax: (65) 6741-2179
inquiries@periplus.com.sg
www.tuttlepublishing.com

TUTTLE PUBLISHING® is a registered trademark of Tuttle Publishing, a division of Periplus Editions (HK) Ltd.